Successful Customer Care
In A Week

Di McLanachan

D0724445

The Teach Yourself series has been trusted around the world
for over 60 years. This series of 'In A Week' business books is
designed to help people at all levels and around the world to
further their careers. Learn in a week, what the experts learn in
a lifetime.

Di McLanachan is managing director of Learning Curves Personal Development Ltd. She is an international trainer, executive coach, a master practitioner of Neuro Linguistic Programming and author of the bestselling book *NLP for Business Excellence*. She has frequently been featured on both radio and television, and has been delivering training in customer care on a regular basis since 1993.

www.learningcurves.co.uk

Successful Customer Care

Di McLanachan

www.inaweek.co.uk

Hodder Education

338 Euston Road, London NW1 3BH.

Hodder Education is an Hachette UK company

First published in UK 1995 by Hodder Education

First published in US 2012 by The McGraw-Hill Companies, Inc.

This edition published 2012.

British Library Cataloguing in Publication Data: a catalogue record for this title is available from the British Library.

Library of Congress Catalog Card Number: on file.

10 9 8 7 6 5 4 3

The publisher has used its best endeavours to ensure that any website addresses referred to in this book are correct and active at the time of going to press. However, the publisher and the author have no responsibility for the websites and can make no guarantee that a site will remain live or that the content will remain relevant, decent or appropriate.

The publisher has made every effort to mark as such all words which it believes to be trademarks. The publisher should also like to make it clear that the presence of a word in the book, whether marked or unmarked, in no way affects its legal status as a trademark.

Every reasonable effort has been made by the publisher to trace the copyright holders of material in this book. Any errors or omissions should be notified in writing to the publisher, who will endeavour to rectify the situation for any reprints and future editions.

Hachette UK's policy is to use papers that are natural, renewable and recyclable products and made from wood grown in sustainable forests. The logging and manufacturing processes are expected to conform to the environmental regulations of the country of origin.

www.hoddereducation.co.uk

Typeset by Cenveo Publisher Services.

Printed and bound by CPI Group (UK) Ltd, Croydon, CR0 4YY.

Contents

Introduction

No matter what type of business you are in, there is one irrefutable fact: if you don't look after your customers, then somebody else will. And that will probably be your competition.

Never before has customer care been such an essential element of any successful, thriving business. Customers no longer have the mentality of 'put up and shut up'; if they're dissatisfied with your product or service, they *will* let you know one way or another. If you're lucky, they will tell you. This is fortunate indeed because it gives you the opportunity of putting right whatever is wrong and compensating the customer for their less than satisfactory experience. If you're unlucky, they will tell you with their feet – by walking away from you and towards an alternative supplier. Along the way, they will probably tell the world and his dog about their bad experience with your organization, and the resulting negative impact on your sales could be significant.

The bottom line is that it costs more to get new customers on board than it does to retain the loyalty, repeat business and recommendations of existing customers. When you focus on keeping your customers happy, there is invariably a positive, knock-on effect on sales. I've seen it happen in organizations where I've run customer care training for their staff and, within just two weeks, sales have taken a distinct upturn.

Even better is the news that customer care doesn't need to cost a lot of money to implement. Often, it's just a matter of mentally 'stepping into the customer's shoes', understanding what they want and putting initiatives in place to deliver what they expect. When you do this, you are achieving 'customer excellence'. You are positioning yourself as a market leader and as a caring organization, and your reputation will draw more business to you.

This book will start you on your journey to becoming a market leader in customer care. We will explore all the different components involved and you will discover that there is far more to it than just how your staff interact with customers.

How do you know what your customers think of you and how can you find out? Feedback is essential in order to ensure that you are focusing on those aspects that are important to your customers. Assumptions won't work; you need to know for certain that any changes you are making are in the right areas – and those areas are determined by your customers.

Communication is such a core skill in customer care that it is vital to get it right. This book incorporates proven Neuro Linguistic Programming (NLP) techniques that will enable you to build a powerful rapport rapidly, whether face to face, over the telephone or even in writing. You will learn about the VHF (visual, hearing, feeling) channels of communication and how to 'tune into your customer's wavelength'. You will even discover how JK Rowling uses this technique in all the Harry Potter books to gain a compelling rapport with her readers.

Most important of all, throughout the book, you will be encouraged to develop your own customer care initiatives to implement within your organization. This ensures that everything you are learning has a practical application and it will enable you to start achieving beneficial results in the shortest time.

SUNDAY

Customer care is more than just saying 'Have a nice day'

It would be very easy to believe that customer care is purely related to how your staff interact with customers and the quality of the service they deliver. However, it is far more than that. Your organization is giving out messages all the time that are interpreted as an attitude towards its customers.

For example, what first impression would a visitor to your organization gain? If you have a reception area, what does it look like? Are there dried-up potted plants, dirty coffee cups and a carpet that clearly hasn't been vacuumed for several days? Or is it clean and tidy, with comfortable seating and perhaps a framed copy of your mission statement on the wall?

Are your reception staff friendly and welcoming or would visitors feel like they are an inconvenience, interrupting a personal conversation by their presence?

What impression does your organization's website convey? Is it difficult to navigate with text errors dotted throughout the pages or does it look sharp, professional and user-friendly?

This chapter intends for you to start thinking about the overall impression that your organization sends out to past, present and potential future customers. In so doing, you will notice that customer care is very closely allied to marketing, in that the image you present is, in effect, your shop window to the world.

Imagine the scene

You're visiting a town that you used to know well some years ago. You haven't been there for a long time but you remember that there used to be a really good Italian restaurant on the high street where you enjoyed many pleasant evenings with fabulous cuisine. You decide that you will seek it out and have a meal there.

You head for the high street, and there is the restaurant, but not quite as you remember it. It looks a little shabby – on the sign outside a letter is missing from the word 'restaurant' so that it now reads 'restaurat'. Undaunted, you step inside. It's quiet – hardly any diners at all. You stand for a few moments, expecting someone to greet you with a smile and usher you to a table. You can see two waiting staff in the distance with their backs to you, chatting and laughing together and completely oblivious to your presence. You decide to approach them and, in fact, you walk right up to them and say, 'Excuse me, table for one, please?' before they are even aware that you exist.

On hearing you speak, they finish their conversation before one of them turns to you, waves an arm in the direction of several unoccupied tables and says, 'Anywhere you like.' You head for a table near the window and become aware that they have resumed their chat. You sit down and take in your surroundings. The lighting is low, and you assume that this is to create an ambience – until you notice that no fewer than

SUNDAY

MONDAY

TUESDAY

WEDNESDAY

THURSDAY

FRIDAY

SATURDAY

five light bulbs have blown and now remain unlit, still in their fittings. On further inspection, you notice the cobwebs that are delicately dangling from the ceiling chandelier.

There is a menu on the table and, despite the large coffee stain on it, the range of dishes on offer looks promising, so you decide to remain optimistic. One of the waiting staff ambles over after you have managed to make eye contact with him. You ask him what the soup of the day is. He hesitates, then turns his head and repeats your question in a raised voice to the waitress, who is now engrossed in sending a text message on her mobile phone. 'Minestrone,' she yells back, without bothering to look up.

You order a bowl of minestrone soup. Fish for your main course would be nice, except that it's off. Chicken, perhaps? No, they've run out of that too. You settle for lasagne and order a glass of wine.

On your table is a small vase of faded silk flowers. The waiter notices you looking at it, picks it up and thoughtfully blows a fine layer of dust off the petals before replacing it before you. 'Thank you,' you hear yourself say as you notice from his fingernails that he probably has a day job as a motor mechanic. In fact, your nose tells you that he must have rushed here straight from the garage without having the time to shower or use a deodorant.

As you sit back in your chair, you look around the room and realize that the décor is exactly the same as it was when you used to come here regularly, all those years ago. Yes, you're certain that this *is* the same wallpaper – it's just not making as much contact with the walls as it used to and one or two pieces are missing altogether.

The waiter returns with your glass of wine and you notice that whoever was last to drink out of this glass had been wearing a delightful shade of rose-pink lipstick.

The soup arrives – a full bowl – and as the waiter plonks it down on the table in front of you, it sloshes over the sides and spills onto the tablecloth. Fortunately, there are already other stains on the cloth so one more won't make any difference. And there's another bonus: there's no need to blow a cooling breath onto every spoonful before putting it in your mouth because it's not too hot at all. In fact, it's lukewarm.

The lasagne is a different prospect completely. Not only is the dish it arrives in far too hot to touch, but the pasta is crisp and curling up at the edges. You suspect it has been reheated in a microwave oven.

By now, your optimism has left you, along with your appetite. You decide to bring this experience to an end and ask for the bill. At least, you would ask for the bill if you could see anyone to ask. The two waiting staff have disappeared now, probably out of the building to have a cigarette.

Finally, you get the bill. You pay in cash, including a small tip that you feel obliged to give, even though the service, and in fact the whole experience, has been abysmal. You leave the money on the table and make for the door, uttering a 'goodbye' on the way there. Behind you is the unmistakeable sound of a deadpan voice saying, 'Have a nice day'.

Although there has been some exaggeration in the details of this story, you may have had a similar experience. You may have felt your heart sink when your favourite pub or restaurant put up a sign saying 'Under New Management'. You may have witnessed standards of care and quality declining, with the inevitable result that customers take their business elsewhere.

So let's explore all the factors that constitute customer care, using the restaurant story as an example.

Visual appearance

- The letter 'n' missing from the word 'restaurant' on the sign outside.
- The five light bulbs that were no longer working.
- Cobwebs dangling from the 'chandelier'.
- The stained tablecloth.
- The coffee stains on the menu.
- The faded silk flowers covered in dust.
- Wallpaper peeling off the walls.

There is a danger that if a problem isn't corrected shortly after it occurs, it starts to become invisible. That is, staff who are constantly around it stop noticing it, as was the case with the items listed above. When a customer arrives, seeing these things for the first time with 'fresh eyes', they form an impression that the business has a slapdash attitude to quality, which probably extends to everything else it does. The customer just might turn on their heel and leave right then.

If your business doesn't have physical premises that a customer would visit, then these principles apply to your website. How professional does it look? Is it easy to find a phone number on there if the customer wants to call you? In particular, check every page with a fine-tooth comb for text errors. I once worked with a family-run cleaning business that relied totally on their website to promote them. Even though they had reviewed every page when it was first created, I found 20 errors spread throughout the site. One in particular sent out an interesting message: instead of the text saying 'we will hoover around you' it read 'we will hover around you'! If your potential customer doesn't like the look of your website, they will leave and look for your competitors' sites instead.

Exercise

Review your organization's visual elements, both physical and virtual, as if you were a potential customer. When reviewing, you are looking at something again, with a greater attention to detail.

Attentiveness and helpfulness of staff

- The two waiting staff chatting instead of noticing a customer approaching.
- The waiter who waved an arm in the direction of some empty tables instead of showing the customer to a specific table.
- The waitress who was busy sending text messages in full view of the customers.
- The waiter didn't know what the soup of the day was.
- Dirty fingernails and lack of personal hygiene.
- Both waiting staff disappeared, probably for a cigarette break.
- The meaningless 'have a nice day' spoken with total insincerity.

Without doubt, staff attitude and behaviour towards customers is the key element in customer care. People buy people first, and even if the food in this restaurant had been superb, the experience was still damaged by the behaviour of the staff.

It is imperative that customer-facing staff *SMILE*. Here are five good reasons why:

1 **Smiling is contagious**. In a study carried out in Sweden, it was discovered that people found it difficult to frown when they were looking at others who were smiling. In fact, their facial muscles started twitching into smiles all on their own! If your staff smile at customers, there is a very strong chance that your customers will smile right back.

2 **Smiling releases endorphins.** Endorphins are the body's natural painkillers and have been found to be anywhere from 18 to 500 times as powerful as any man-made analgesic. Endorphins are non-addictive, can reduce feelings of stress and frustration and can even control cravings for chocolate and potentially addictive substances. In fact, they are the best (and legal) way to achieve a natural 'high'.

3 **Smiling boosts your mood**. Because the mind and body are inextricably linked, psychologists have found that even a forced smile will instantly lift your spirits. So smiling staff really are happy staff.

4 **Smiling is easier than frowning**. Your body has to work much harder and use far more muscles to produce a frown than to smile. Also, frowning is ageing whereas smiling lifts the face and makes you look younger.

5 **A smile can be heard over the telephone**. If you change the shape of your mouth, the voice coming out of it will sound different. Even if you can't see your customer, you can still smile at them down the phone and they *will* be able to hear that.

Quality of the product or service

● Lukewarm soup.
● Menu choices not available.
● Lasagne microwaved to a crisp.

SUNDAY
MONDAY
TUESDAY
WEDNESDAY
THURSDAY
FRIDAY
SATURDAY

In the restaurant example, the food would have needed to be outstandingly good to compensate for everything else that was lacking. It wasn't. And I'm sure our customer never set foot in there again.

However, people often behave in an interesting way in restaurants. Perhaps you've had it happen that you and a companion order your meal, it arrives and, while you're eating, you both comment that the quality isn't as good as it could be. Just then, the waiter appears and asks if everything is okay and you hear yourself saying, 'Yes, fine, thank you'. Perhaps you don't want to make a fuss, and what could the waiter do about it anyway? So you say nothing, but you take your custom elsewhere. The waiter, who hasn't personally tasted the food he put in front of you, is unaware that there is a quality issue. He only knows that the restaurant doesn't get as busy as it used to, but assumes that this is just a sign of the present 'economic climate' out there.

It is very, very important to not only maintain your existing standards of quality but also seek continuous improvement. It's too easy to become complacent, to unwittingly allow standards to slip and then have the uphill struggle of trying to recover your previous good reputation and tempt 'lost' customers to return to you. Even from an economic standpoint, it costs more to get new customers on board than it does to retain existing ones. Get your customer care right and you can reduce your marketing costs.

Summary

In this chapter, we have explored some of the many components of customer care. We've seen that it is not just about how the staff conduct themselves; it is also about how the organization conducts itself.

We have highlighted three key focus areas – visual appearance, attentiveness and helpfulness of staff, and quality of product or service. They work well as starting points for achieving excellent customer care.

What are your competitors doing in these three areas? If you've ever lost even one customer to a competitor, why was that? You need to know what your competitors are doing, how they're doing it and how you can do it even better. This is valuable *research*; every organization does it.

Competition is the best incentive there can be to keep you on your toes with customer care. It can give you ideas for quality initiatives that you wouldn't otherwise have thought of – you may not be in the same industry, but could their ideas 'map across' to you?

Fact-check (answers at the back)

1. Which statement is true?
   a) The visual appearance of your business makes no difference to customer perceptions. ❏
   b) Attention to detail is nit-picking, time wasting and unnecessary. ❏
   c) Customers see your business with 'fresh eyes' and notice things you don't see. ❏
   d) The cleanliness of your business premises is of little importance. ❏

2. Which statement is true?
   a) It costs more to keep existing customers happy than it does to attract new customers. ❏
   b) It costs more to generate new customers than it does to retain existing ones. ❏
   c) Customers are naturally loyal and will always overlook your failings. ❏
   d) Customer care and marketing are completely separate functions. ❏

3. Which statement is true?
   a) Nobody will notice the occasional text error in your website. ❏
   b) A website is just a marketing tool; it has nothing to do with customer care. ❏
   c) As long as you have a website, you don't need to publish your phone number. ❏

   d) Your website is your organization's shop window to the world. ❏

4. Which statement is true?
   a) Personal appearance and hygiene are very important for customer-facing staff. ❏
   b) If staff don't feel like being attentive to customers, they needn't be. ❏
   c) 'Have a nice day' always works well, spoken in any tone of voice. ❏
   d) As long as you have wished your customer a nice day, you have fulfilled all your customer care responsibilities. ❏

5. Which statement is true?
   a) Customer care begins and ends with your customer-facing staff. ❏
   b) Customer care is about how your staff and your organization conduct themselves. ❏
   c) Customer care is a nice idea that will probably just happen anyway. ❏
   d) Customers are an inconvenience and interruption to the working day. ❏

13

MONDAY

How do you measure up?

If I were to ask you how your organization is performing, you would probably refer me to the last set of annual accounts. You would be able to give me figures for annual turnover, gross profit, net profit and so on. Departments within your organization will have budgets allocated to them, within which they must contain all their operating expenses. No doubt, they track actual against planned on an ongoing basis so that any remedial actions can be taken as appropriate.

In short, because money is tangible and relatively easy to measure, it gets measured. However, it should be said that a set of accounts can only ever represent past performance – like looking in a rear-view mirror while driving forward.

Customer care is less tangible than money, and therefore it is not as easy to measure. Because of this, it often gets overlooked as a measure of performance. Managers are unlikely to have a monthly or yearly plan for customer care against which their actual performance can be measured, yet if any department significantly underperforms in this area, there could potentially be a serious impact to the organization's financial results.

In this chapter, we will explore ways of creating and implementing customer service standards throughout your organization to nurture a consistent, conscientious approach to customer care.

Common sense

Customer care should just be a matter of common sense; it is, after all, about treating others in the way you would like to be treated. How difficult can that be? However, what is common sense to one person is not common sense to another, hence the need for standards.

If your business is engaged in the manufacture of a product, then you probably already have quality standards in place, for example ISO 9001. But do you also have customer service standards to supplement these? The British Standards Institution has published a Customer Service Code of Practice, BS 8477, which is intended for guidance and recommendation rather than being a compliance document.

If your business is service based, then the quality of your customer service is key to the operating success of your organization. According to the Institute of Customer Service (ICS), service standards 'help to define what a customer can expect and remind management and employees of the challenge and obligations that they face'. The ICS goes on to recommend that service standards need to be defined in terms of the following three areas:

- timeliness
- accuracy
- appropriateness.

Let's look at each of these in turn, and explore exactly what they mean.

Timeliness

A common measure of timeliness is the promptness of answering telephones. Many organizations pledge that phones will be answered within three rings and, while this is a very noble idea, it implies that this will happen 100 per cent of the time, which isn't always possible. Working days and working hours need to be taken into consideration when setting standards, and defining an acceptable 'success percentage' is better than implying that nothing less than 100 per cent will do.

For example, 'During our working hours of 8.30 a.m. to 5.30 p.m. on weekdays, 95 per cent of calls will be answered within three rings'. This is a perfectly acceptable service standard.

If yours is an organization that promises 'next day delivery' then this implies that it includes weekends and that delivery can be to anywhere in the world. If this isn't the case, then 'next day' needs to be more specific, for example weekdays only and UK mainland only (if you are a UK-based business).

It is also a good idea to have a performance standard for your customer-facing staff on how long it should take to resolve a customer's problem. Although many problems can be dealt with during the course of a telephone conversation, more complex ones may require investigation, possibly involving staff from other parts of the organization.

Once a complaint or problem has been registered by a customer, the clock is ticking. Whether they have reported it to you verbally, in writing or via email, they now have an expectation that somebody is dealing with it and that it has been given an appropriate level of importance – high! If the problem is a complex one, requiring more time to investigate than a couple of hours at the most, it is essential that the customer is kept up to date with progress, even if that progress is minimal. The customer who hears nothing will feel neglected, and if they already have a grievance with you this will fan the flames and make it much worse.

Accuracy

Unlike timeliness, where accuracy is concerned nothing less than 100 per cent is acceptable. Imagine that you have had a consultation with your doctor for an ailment. He has given you a prescription but, unfortunately, he made a small error in spelling the name of the medication and you are about to be given something completely different by the pharmacist. At worst, this alternative medication could be harmful, or even dangerous, to you. The fact that 98 per cent of your doctor's service was accurate just wouldn't be good enough; it must be 100 per cent to be acceptable.

Customers expect 100 per cent accuracy on everything, especially in the following areas:

● the spelling of their name
● their address details
● the delivery date and time promised

- invoice or receipt details, especially amount charged
- goods or services to exactly match their description and be reliable
- information or promises given, either verbally or in writing
- the goods delivered match exactly what was ordered.

Exercise

Do you have any processes or procedures in place to check the accuracy of the product or service you supply to customers? If so, what are they?

....

....

....

What percentage of accuracy are you currently achieving and how do you know that?

....

....

Define three service standards related to accuracy that either already exist within your organization or would improve your customer care if they did exist:

1. ....
2. ....
3. ....

Appropriateness

This relates to how well you meet your customers' expectations, particularly when responding to enquiries or complaints. For example, you have ordered goods via the internet and you receive a partial delivery. You send an email to the supplier asking when you can expect the remainder of the delivery and whether this split delivery will affect the 14-day free trial that was promised when you placed your order. You receive a reply that anticipated delivery will be in ten days' time, with an apology for the delay. That's it – no mention of the 14-day free trial at all. The level of appropriateness demonstrated by the supplier was a dismal 50 per cent and you now feel that you have to email them again, to restate your question about the trial period.

Exercise

Do you have any processes or procedures in place to check the appropriateness of responses your organization makes to customers? If so, what are they?

....
....
....

What percentage of appropriateness are you currently achieving and how do you know that?

....
....

Define three service standards related to appropriateness that either already exist within your organization or would improve your customer care if they did exist.

1. ....
2. ....
3. ....

Writing service standards

When writing service standards, ensure that they are defined precisely and concisely, with no ambiguity that would allow for any misunderstanding or misinterpretation. Also think about how each service standard can be implemented and measured. This will ensure that they are realistic and serve a valuable purpose in confirming that your customers really are receiving a high and consistent standard of care.

At this point, it is worth getting input from other sources as to the areas that need to be included in your service standards, for example:

● management at all levels
● staff, especially customer-facing staff

- customers
- potential future customers
- previous customers (why are they no longer your customers?)
- competitors (remember this is research, not spying)
- any regulatory authorities relevant to your industry.

Implementing service standards

So, you've written them and they are comprehensive and clear – now what? There needs to be ownership throughout all levels of your organization, starting at the very top. The standards need to be cascaded down to all staff, and perhaps included in everyone's job objectives, so that each individual is evaluated on how well he or she performs in relation to these standards at their annual appraisal.

Visibility of the standards can be maintained through your organization's internal communication channels, e.g. newsletters, notice boards, intranet, discussion at department meetings and so on. Externally, this visibility can be turned into a real, public commitment to customer service by including a reference to service standards in the mission, vision or values of the organization.

The following are examples of organizations that have done just this.

Low-cost airline **Easyjet**'s mission statement:

> *To provide our customers with safe, good value, point-to-point air services. To effect and to offer a consistent and reliable product and fares appealing to leisure and business markets on a range of European routes. To achieve this we will develop our people and establish lasting relationships with our suppliers.*

McDonald's vision:

> *To be the world's best quick service restaurant experience. Being the best means providing outstanding quality, service, cleanliness, and value, so that we make every customer in every restaurant smile.*

The Home Depot's mission statement:

The Home Depot is in the home improvement business and our goal is to provide the highest level of service, the broadest selection of products and the most competitive prices. We are a values-driven company and our eight core values include the following:

1. Excellent customer service

2. Taking care of our people

3. Giving back

4. Doing the 'right' thing

5. Creating shareholder value

6. Respect for all people

7. Entrepreneurial spirit

8. Building strong relationships

Avon Cosmetics' mission statement:

The Global Beauty Leader

We will build a unique portfolio of beauty and related brands, striving to surpass our competitors in quality, innovation and value, and elevating our image to become the beauty company most women turn to worldwide.

The Women's Choice for Buying

We will become the destination store for women, offering the convenience of multiple brands and channels, and providing a personal high touch shopping experience that helps create lifelong customer relationships.

The Premier Direct Seller

We will expand our presence in direct selling and lead the reinvention of the channel, offering an entrepreneurial opportunity that delivers superior earnings, recognition, service and support, making it easy and rewarding to be affiliated with Avon and elevating the image of our industry.

The Best Place to Work

We will be known for our leadership edge, through our passion for high standards, our respect for diversity and our commitment to create exceptional opportunities for professional growth so that associates can fulfil their highest potential.

The Largest Women's Foundation

We will be a committed global champion for the health and well-being of women through philanthropic efforts that eliminate breast cancer from the face of the earth, and that empower women to achieve economic independence.

The Most Admired Company

We will deliver superior returns to our shareholders by tirelessly pursuing new growth opportunities while continually improving our profitability, a socially responsible, ethical company that is watched and emulated as a model of success.

Estee Lauder's mission statement:

The guiding vision of The Estee Lauder Companies is 'Bringing the best to everyone we touch'. By 'The best', we mean the best products, the best people and the best ideas. These three pillars have been the hallmarks of our Company since it was founded by Mrs Estee Lauder in 1946. They remain the foundation upon which we continue to build our success today.

Barnes & Nobles bookstores:

Our mission is to operate the best specialty retail business in America, regardless of the product we sell. Because the product we sell is books, our aspirations must be consistent with the promise and the ideals of the volumes which line our shelves. To say that our mission exists independent of the product we sell is to demean the importance and the distinction of being booksellers. As booksellers we are determined to be the very best in our business, regardless of the size, pedigree or inclinations of our competitors. We will continue to bring our industry nuances of style and approaches to bookselling which are consistent with our evolving aspirations. Above all, we expect to be a credit to the communities we serve, a valuable resource to our customers, and a place where our dedicated booksellers can grow and prosper. Toward this end we will not only listen to our customers and booksellers but embrace the idea that the Company is at their service.

The **MBNA Corporation** (a financial institution and holding company that is also an independent credit card lender. Its three primary banks are the MBNA America Bank, MBNA Europe Bank and the MBNA Canada Bank):

Our mission is to provide you with an outstanding member/Customer benefit that helps you meet your organization's objectives. We work very hard to understand your objectives, then create a program that can help you meet them. Whether you want to attract new members, retain existing ones, drive incremental sales, or reinforce member or brand loyalty, we will work with you to help you achieve those goals.

Microsoft's mission statement:

At Microsoft, we work to help people and businesses throughout the world realize their full potential. This is our mission. Everything we do reflects this mission and the values that make it possible.

Once service standards have been created and made public, it is essential that *everyone* in your organization 'walks the talk'. It's very easy for those staff who perceive themselves to be more 'back room' than customer facing to believe that customer service standards don't apply to them. And yet it's quite feasible that an incoming call might get put through to a department that doesn't usually deal directly with customers. The phone might be left to ring for a minute or two, before someone finally picks it up and snaps, 'Yeah?'. Your carefully thought out service standard of answering within three rings with 'Good morning, [name] speaking, how may I help you?' has just gone out the window.

Customer service is everyone's business, from the Chief Executive Officer through to the cleaning staff. Whenever I stay in a hotel, I'm always impressed by the cleaners I encounter who deliberately make eye contact with me, smile and say 'Good morning' in a genuinely courteous tone of voice. For me, this enhances the entire hotel experience and speaks volumes about the standards of customer service that must be in place. I would quite happily stay at that hotel again and I'd recommend it to others.

Line managers play an important role in nurturing a 'customer-friendly' attitude in their staff, and often this attitude plays a key part in selection criteria at recruitment interviews. If the culture of an organization is one of serving customers, and enjoying doing it, then not only does this generate a positive reputation externally, it also creates a happy, motivating work environment internally. This in turn decreases staff turnover, with the financial benefits of reduced recruitment and training costs.

Many organizations use motivational posters displayed on, for example, notice boards to continually remind staff of the importance of maintaining a focus on customer service. Typical slogans include 'If we don't look after our customers, somebody else will'. You may have seen posters like this; although the words may seem a bit trite, the message is clear and to the point.

Summary

In this chapter, we have looked at ways in which you can define appropriate levels of customer service and incorporate them into standards that will apply throughout your organization. It is always useful to know what other organizations similar to yours are including in their standards, and conducting research on this topic can provide you with ideas and other sources of inspiration for writing your own.

The important point is that your standards must be visible to, and understood by, staff at all levels in your organization. For example, if you define a procedure for resolving customer complaints within a specified period of time and one of your employees misses this deadline because he or she didn't know it existed, then communication of the standard has been ineffective and needs to be addressed. Your organization's culture must be 'walk the talk', and going public on this in a mission statement indicates to the world that you really are serious about it.

And one final point – if you are in the business of selling products, then you and your staff need to be fully conversant with the Sale of Goods Act and all the legalities it contains, particularly related to warranties. This is one standard that is not optional!

Fact-check (answers at the back)

1. Your company's annual accounts represent:
   - a) Day-to-day trading figures ❏
   - b) Future market trends ❏
   - c) Past financial performance ❏
   - d) Planned versus actual expenditure ❏

2. Customer care is:
   - a) A 'nice to have' option ❏
   - b) A performance measurement ❏
   - c) Only applicable to customer-facing staff ❏
   - d) Not relevant to your organization ❏

3. Which statement is true?
   - a) Only manufacturing businesses need to have standards in place. ❏
   - b) Everyone has common sense so there is no need to define service standards in writing. ❏
   - c) Customer care is as tangible as money. ❏
   - d) Service standards remind all levels of staff of their customer care obligations. ❏

4. It is recommended that service standards be defined in terms of:
   - a) Timeliness, accuracy, profit margins ❏
   - b) Timeliness, accuracy, appropriateness ❏
   - c) Timeliness, dress code, appropriateness ❏
   - d) Reputation, accuracy, appropriateness ❏

5. Which statement is true?
   - a) Telephones *must* be answered within three rings at all times. ❏
   - b) 'Next day delivery' needs to be clarified to avoid misunderstandings. ❏
   - c) As long as the phone gets answered eventually, the customer has been served. ❏
   - d) Problem resolution can take a long time and the customer should be patient. ❏

6. The acceptable percentage for accuracy is:
   - a) 100 per cent ❏
   - b) 98 per cent ❏
   - c) 95 per cent ❏
   - d) 93 per cent ❏

7. Which statement is true?
   - a) If people have an unusual name, they should expect it to get spelt wrongly. ❏
   - b) A delivery date is just an estimate, not a promise. ❏
   - c) If a product is similar to its description, that is good enough. ❏
   - d) Goods must match exactly what was ordered by the customer. ❏

8. Which statement is true?
a) Appropriateness relates to your tone of voice when dealing with a customer. ❏
b) Appropriateness relates to how well you meet your customers' expectations. ❏
c) As long as the customer has received a response of some kind, appropriateness has been achieved. ❏
d) By the nature of their role, customer-facing staff are automatically 'appropriate'. ❏

9. Which statement is true?
a) Service standards need to be defined precisely and concisely. ❏
b) Implementation and measurement need not be considered at this stage. ❏
c) Input from past customers has no value. ❏
d) There is nothing to be learnt from competitors. ❏

10. Which statement is true?
a) As long as standards have been written, that is good enough. ❏
b) Senior management are too far removed from customers to bother with maintaining standards. ❏
c) Visibility of service standards to all levels of staff in an organization is essential. ❏
d) A mission statement is not the appropriate place for customer service standards to be made public. ❏

SUNDAY

MONDAY

TUESDAY

WEDNESDAY

THURSDAY

FRIDAY

SATURDAY

How do your customers think you measure up?

In the previous chapter, the focus was on creating your own set of customer service standards and then measuring your organization's performance against them. This is, of course, good customer care practice.

Here's the bad news. No matter how well you have defined your standards and are monitoring performance, your customers will always decide what your *real* standards are. You might hate the phrase 'the customer is always right', but your customers are your reality check. You might be consistently achieving the standards you have put in place, but if your customers have a different set of standards against which they are evaluating you, then yours are obsolete.

It is also a bad idea to assume that 'no news is good news'. I have lost count of the number of times I have worked with organizations that had adopted the attitude of believing their product or service must be acceptable because 'nobody's complained yet'. Customers will not necessarily complain in words; it is more likely that they will complain with their feet (by walking away from you).

It is essential that you find out what your customers think of you – don't assume, ask them. You need this information to get a clear understanding of how you are *really* performing and also to identify areas for improvement. This chapter explores the ways in which you can do this effectively and how this in turn can enhance customer loyalty and even bring you new customers.

SUNDAY MONDAY TUESDAY WEDNESDAY THURSDAY FRIDAY SATURDAY

How well do you know your customers?

Who is your typical customer? Are they an individual or an organization? Do they buy from you face to face or via the internet? These are questions that you should know the answers to, and the following is a customer profiling exercise to check out just how well you know them.

Exercise

There are two sections to this profiling questionnaire: the first relates to individuals and the second relates to organizations. You might have both types of customer buying from you, in which case complete both sections. If, however, your customers are predominantly one type or the other, then complete only the appropriate section.

- Individual customers
  - Gender ....
  - Age ....
  - Family ....
  - Where they live ....
  - Employment ....
  - Approximate income ....
  - Hobbies/interests ....
  - Aspirations/goals ....
  - What they buy from you ....
  - How often do they buy? ....
- Organizations
  - Size (number of staff) ....
  - Annual turnover ....
  - Location ....
  - Number of years established ....
  - Nature of business ....
  - Purchasing procedure ....
  - Decision maker ....
  - What they buy from you ....
  - How often do they buy? ....

If you are answering the organization questions, 'purchasing procedure' relates to the process for making a purchase. For example, does someone within the organization raise a request for purchase and a buyer from the procurement department then approaches three potential suppliers for a quotation? Is there an approved suppliers list and, if so, how often is it reviewed? Is the buyer also the decision maker or is someone else in the organization responsible for the final sign-off? If you are dealing with organizations as your main source of business, then you need to know all these things.

The following questions relate to both individuals and organizations as customers:

● How did they find out about you?

....
....

● What is important to them in dealing with you?

....
....

● What exactly do they expect from you?

....
....

● How well are you meeting their expectations?

....
....

● How do you know that?

....

....

● How might their expectations and needs change in the future?

....

....

What you have been doing in this exercise is, effectively, stepping into the shoes of your (typical) customer. If you found this hard to do, then you may not be as attuned to your customers as you need to be. This particularly relates to the questions about how well you are meeting their expectations and how you know that. If you made assumptions when you answered those questions, then the real answer is that you *don't know* how well you are meeting your customers' expectations. *You need to know.*

You particularly need to know if your customers are dissatisfied for any reason. The following iceberg model illustrates the importance of this.

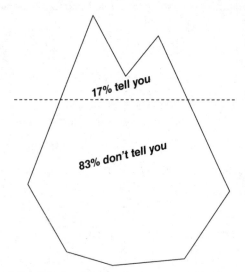

The iceberg of dissatisfied customers

Of all your dissatisfied customers, only 17 per cent (above the water line) will actually tell you that they are unhappy, giving you the opportunity to put things right. They, in turn, will each tell an average of five other people about their experience with you, so *85 people get a positive message* about how you look after your customers, even if something has not been quite right.

The remaining 83 per cent (below the water line) say nothing to you about their dissatisfaction, so you have no opportunity to take remedial action. However, on average, they each tell nine other people that their experience with you was a bad one, so *747 people hear a negative story* about you.

The moral of the story is that it wasn't the tip of the iceberg that sank the *Titanic* – it was the mass below the water line. You need to know about *all* of your dissatisfied customers so that you can resolve their problems and ensure that only positive messages about you are passed on to other potential customers.

Finding out what your customers think of you

There are several ways that you can ask your customers for feedback. For example:

- asking them face to face immediately after business has been transacted
- giving them a feedback card or form to complete which they can either give back to you there and then or post back to you later
- writing to them with a survey form for them to complete and send back
- emailing them with an online survey for them to complete
- telephoning them to ask for feedback over the phone
- using a market research company to collect and analyse feedback.

It is essential that your customers feel that their feedback is important and will be taken seriously. You could confirm to them that you might well make changes for the better in the future, based on their input and suggestions. In so doing, your customers feel valued and are more likely to remain your customers.

Have you ever stayed in a hotel where there was a customer feedback form or card in your room with a request that you fill it out and either hand it in to reception when you check out or post back later?

Have you ever stayed in a hotel where, in your room, there was a short summary of changes the hotel had made in the last six months as a result of reviewing and acting upon feedback from guests who had completed the feedback form?

You may well have answered 'yes' to the first question, but what about the second question? Many hotels just pay 'lip service' to the concept of gathering feedback from their guests. But just imagine that you stayed at a particular hotel and took the time and trouble to complete a feedback form, and when you happened to stay there again a few months later, you discovered that a suggestion you had made had been implemented. Even better, when you reached your room, you found a personalised note from the manager, thanking you for the previous suggestion you had made, confirming that it had been implemented and welcoming any further ideas you might have. How valued would you feel? How happy would you be to stay there again in the future? And how many people might you tell about this?

So, as you can see, the benefits of getting feedback from your customers go well beyond just finding out what they think of you. Customer loyalty can be enhanced and new customers gained through referrals.

What information do you ask for?

Start with deciding what you really want to find out about. You could compose countless questions about product quality, speed of service, politeness of staff and so on; however, a feedback form that is so lengthy it has become intimidating and time-consuming is less likely to get completed.

The two essential things that you need to know about are:

1 What is it about your product or service that is important to your customers?
2 How well are you delivering on those important areas?

Let's imagine for a moment that you are a manufacturer of mobile phones. You have decided to bring out a new, enhanced model and you believe that your customers just love to have a large range of ringtones to choose from, so you invest time and money in creating some new ones. When you announce the launch of your new model, incorporating the increased range of ringtones as a marketing and customer care tool, you are disappointed to find that the volume of sales is less than you had anticipated.

At around the same time, a competitor of yours also announces the launch of a new mobile phone, and their main promotional feature is a battery with a significantly extended life. Their sales go through the roof. Why? Because they took the time and trouble to find out what mobile phone features are important to their customers and then supplied them. You assumed that ringtones were important; your customers would have told you that battery life was more important, if you had but asked them.

Although there is no definitive template for a feedback form, the following are extracts taken from real examples of satisfaction survey forms issued by a variety of different businesses. In each case, the intentions behind the questions are good; however, the final format is less than ideal. The names of the businesses have been withheld; they are identified by their industry type. I have reproduced the actual text from the forms with my comments shown in normal text throughout.

Supermarket

Where appropriate, the card asks for a tick in one of five boxes, ranging from poor to excellent.

> *We would like your comments*
> What do you think of our prices?
> What can you buy cheaper elsewhere?
> What have you particularly liked about shopping here recently?
> Is there anything you have disliked about shopping here recently?

Overall, how do you rate us at satisfying all your everyday shopping needs?

Day and time of visit

Your postcode

Please post this card in the 'We're listening' post box or hand it in at the customer services desk.

We are unable to reply to individual comments. For urgent issues, please contact customer services. Thanks for your help.

Considering this card is headed 'We would like your comments' and a post box labelled 'We're listening' is provided, it is very disappointing that this supermarket is refusing to respond to individual comments. The card continues on the other side with:

Please tick the relevant boxes . . .
(from poor to excellent)

Products:
- Choice/range
- Always able to get the products you want
- Quality
- Finding products easily
- Any comments about specific products
- What other products would you like us to provide?

Staff:
- Helpfulness of our staff
- Speed of service at checkout

Store:
- Store cleanliness and tidiness
- Ease of parking
- Finding the trolley you want

Customers are invited to list other products they would like to see in the store, but because the supermarket is not prepared to respond to these requests, the customer may assume that the product they have requested will now be stocked, and be disappointed if it isn't.

It is interesting that the only personal information the card requests is the day and time of visit and the customer's postcode. Presumably, the store is planning to carry out an analysis of how far people travel to do their grocery shopping and at what time of day. If they had asked for the customer's name and a contact telephone number, they could have offered a prize draw for a £50 voucher to spend in the store. This would have been an incentive to fill in the card and would have demonstrated that customers' input is valuable.

Car dealership

A six-page A4-sized document posted to customers three weeks after servicing is carried out.

> How satisfied were you with your recent service experience at the dealership? Please score your level of satisfaction on a scale of 1.0 (completely dissatisfied) to 5.0 (completely satisfied) in the boxes opposite.
>
> For example, if fairly satisfied you might provide a score of 3.2 or if you are completely satisfied you might provide a score of 5.0.

The length of this survey is intimidating enough; however, the questions in the first section ask for a response in decimals, which is unnecessary. A score between 1 and 5 is sufficient; getting into decimals is too precise and nit-picky.

The next five sections of the form ask for your evaluation by ticking one of five boxes, which are:

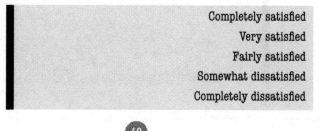

> Completely satisfied
> Very satisfied
> Fairly satisfied
> Somewhat dissatisfied
> Completely dissatisfied

This is inconsistent. Either they want precise scores with decimal points or they want evaluations based on the headings above. A mixture of the two on the same form gives the impression that there were at least two authors of this document, who had a disagreement. The only way to resolve their conflict was a compromise, and hence the two completely different ways of scoring. This really doesn't give a good impression to the customer. The form continues with:

How satisfied were you with . . .

- The ease of getting through to the dealership to book an appointment?
- The ease of getting a service appointment within a reasonable time?
- The dealership's ability to give you an appointment for the date/time you requested?
- The appearance of the dealer's service department?
- The ease of parking when you visited the dealership?
- The waiting time when you dropped off your car?
- The friendliness/helpfulness of the service advisor?
- The service advisor's ability to understand your individual issues?
- The technical competence of the service advisor?
- Their ability to provide a cost estimate?
- The dealer's ability to offer an alternative method of transport (if required)?
- Their ability to complete the work within the timescales given?
- The availability of all necessary parts?
- The quality of the work performed?
- The level of contact to keep you updated while your vehicle was being serviced?

And so it goes on. On the positive side, the covering letter that accompanies this form does promise that if it is completed and returned in the postage-paid envelope provided by a specific date, the customer will be entered into a prize draw to win a 'luxury break' at a smart hotel. This is a good incentive and, in light of the length of the survey, absolutely necessary to encourage the customer to spend time working through this tedious form.

Hospital accident and emergency department

A double-sided, almost A4-sized card, headed 'satisfaction survey'.

> We are constantly striving to improve the quality of the Accident and Emergency (A&E) service. You can help us to do this by filling in the questionnaire on the other side of this card. The cards are collected each day and the results analysed. Your opinions will help to shape the future of the Accident Centre.
>
> Indicate your opinion by marking the appropriate box with a straight line, like this: —

This is really helpful if you have no idea what a straight line looks like!

> Please use a pencil or blue/black pen.

Now you're in trouble. You just came along here with your broken leg. You had no idea that you needed to have your pencil case with you!

> Mark only one box for each question and rub out any mistakes.

What if you've been using a pen? Should have brought along your pencils *and* an eraser!

> Please post the completed card in the box, to the right of the door leading out of the department. Do not fold, bend or tear this card.

A bit optimistic – might depend on the state you're in when you're finally ready to leave A&E. Some of the questions can't be answered until then.

The next section provides options of:

● Not applicable
● Very good
● Good
● Acceptable
● Poor
● Very poor

> What was your experience of the following:
>
> • Waiting time to register
> • Waiting time to see the doctor
> • Waiting time for X-ray
> • Waiting time for treatment
> • Staff courtesy – nurse
> • Staff courtesy – doctor
> • Effectiveness of the anaesthetic
> • Information from staff
> • Quality of treatment
> • Appearance of department

I love the question about effectiveness of the anaesthetic! If it worked particularly well, you may be so woozy that you're having trouble finding the door out of A&E, let alone the post box for your card! However, if it didn't work too well and you've been sitting around waiting for some time in considerable pain, you have very likely ripped this card into small pieces by now.

The final section gives options of Agree, Disagree and Don't know.

> Do you agree with the following aspects of the centre's policy?
>
> - Children under 12 receive priority care for non-urgent conditions
> - Trained nurses manage minor conditions (no doctor involved)
> - Background music in the waiting room

Interestingly, it doesn't actually state what the centre's policies are with respect to these points. For example, if there is no background music playing, does that mean that this is their policy or does it mean that there should be music playing but something has gone wrong?

Summary

In this chapter, we have explored the importance of getting feedback from your customers as to how they believe you are performing. If you make assumptions about what your customers think about you and what their needs are, there will always be at least a 50 per cent chance that your assumptions are incorrect. Your customers are your life blood – you need to know how to keep them satisfied in order to retain their loyalty.

The following are key points to bear in mind when formulating a customer satisfaction survey:

● Determine exactly what you want to find out and include only those questions that will give you that result.

● You need to know what is important to your customers and how they feel you are performing in those areas.

● Avoid making your survey form too long – it becomes tedious and won't get completed.

● If you are posting forms out to your customers, you *must* include a pre-paid envelope for their return.

SUNDAY
MONDAY
TUESDAY
WEDNESDAY
THURSDAY
FRIDAY
SATURDAY

- Offering an incentive such as a prize draw or complimentary voucher will encourage your customers to complete a survey.

- If you have asked for suggestions, then you need to acknowledge them; otherwise, there will be an expectation that all suggestions will be implemented.

- When you've analysed results, find a way to publish them. This will make everyone who participated in the survey feel valued, as well as being a good public relations exercise for you.

Before reading any further, this is a good point at which to put together a draft version of a satisfaction survey. In addition to your own ideas, you could also ask for others' input and suggestions, ensuring that it retains a conciseness in its final form.

Fact-check (answers at the back)

1. Which statement is true?
   a) Your competitors define your service standards. ❏
   b) Your service standards will always be the same as your customers' standards. ❏
   c) Your customers define the standards you need to meet. ❏
   d) As long as nobody is complaining, your standards are good enough. ❏

2. Which statement is true?
   a) 17 per cent of dissatisfied customers don't complain. ❏
   b) 83 per cent of dissatisfied customers complain loudly. ❏
   c) The customers who don't complain each tell five others about your poor service. ❏
   d) You can only resolve problems that your customers tell you about. ❏

3. Which statement is true?
   a) You need to know what your customers expect from you. ❏
   b) You probably know how well you are meeting their expectations. ❏
   c) Your customers' future needs will be the same as they are now. ❏
   d) Your customers must be happy if you don't hear anything negative from them. ❏

4. Which statement is true?
   a) Feedback from customers is of little importance to your business. ❏
   b) Feedback from customers contributes to planning the future of your business. ❏
   c) Customers don't need to know whether their feedback will be taken seriously. ❏
   d) As long as you smile at your customers, they will feel valued. ❏

5. Which statement is true?
   a) It is important to know how far your customers travel to do business with you. ❏
   b) People don't like being asked for their opinions. ❏
   c) You need to know what is important to your customers about your product or service. ❏
   d) There is no need to acknowledge suggestions put forward by your customers. ❏

6. Which statement is true?
a) As long as your prices are competitive, nothing else matters to your customers. ❏
b) If you think a particular aspect of your product/service should be important to your customers, then it will be. ❏
c) People need no incentives to encourage them to fill out lengthy satisfaction surveys. ❏
d) Responding positively to customer feedback can contribute to an organization's business success. ❏

7. Which statement is true?
a) Mixing different methods of scoring on a satisfaction survey is not good practice. ❏
b) People should expect to pay postage costs to return a completed survey form. ❏
c) The point of asking customers to give feedback is purely for your organization to look as if it cares. ❏
d) No customer would ever expect their suggestions to be implemented. ❏

8. Which statement is true?
a) Customers are just an inconvenience. ❏
b) Your customers are your life blood. ❏
c) Your customers shouldn't expect so much of you. ❏
d) Your customers are always wrong. ❏

9. Which statement is true?
a) If you make assumptions, they will always be correct. ❏
b) Product improvements based on assumptions may not represent the best investment of your time and money. ❏
c) There is a 70 per cent chance of an assumption being correct. ❏
d) The possible margin for error in an assumption is 20 per cent. ❏

10. Which statement is true?
a) Customers are not interested in seeing the results of a survey in which they have participated. ❏
b) Customers have no expectations related to service. ❏
c) It is okay to take customer loyalty for granted. ❏
d) People are more likely to complete a survey form if there is a chance of winning a prize as a result. ❏

SUNDAY
MONDAY
TUESDAY
WEDNESDAY
THURSDAY
FRIDAY
SATURDAY

WEDNESDAY

Delivering more than your customers expect

In the previous chapter, we explored how your customers define your service standards by their expectations, and it is their expectations that you need to fulfil in order to achieve a good standard of customer care. In this chapter, we will 'boldly go' beyond your customers' expectations and discover how to delight them by achieving customer excellence.

It is by consistently exceeding others' expectations that you not only retain your customers, but turn them into your 'raving fans'. The real bonus of this is that they will then do your marketing for you, by telling their friends, family and anyone else who is remotely interested that you are the best thing since sliced bread. Because people like to buy from people they know, like and trust, such 'referral marketing' is particularly effective. It also helps to build and sustain your reputation as an organization that really cares about its customers.

One of the key principles at work in achieving customer excellence is to under-promise and over-deliver. Even though your mission statement might encapsulate your customer service standards, by maintaining an attitude of constantly over-delivering on those standards you will build a reputation of outstanding customer care.

Included in this chapter are examples of organizations that have achieved, and continue to achieve, customer excellence. There are, of course, many more and, as you are reading this, others may come to mind for you. If so, notice exactly what it is that is generating this level of excellence, and whether there are any ideas that you could replicate for yourself and your organization.

Excellence doesn't need to cost a lot of money

Many years ago, I was recommended a stationery supplier that guaranteed next day delivery free of charge for all orders over £30 in value. They would also offer free gifts such as a box of envelopes, a pack of A4-sized writing pads, a personal CD player and so on. I started buying my stationery from them on a regular basis and found them to be very reliable and good value for money.

One January, during an outbreak of influenza, I rang in a stationery order and was told that I would also receive a free ream of photocopy paper. Sure enough, the next day, when my order was delivered and I unpacked all the items I had ordered, I was pleased to find the promised free ream of paper. However, the box wasn't empty. Down in one corner was a pack of three tubes of medicated throat sweets – not ordered, not expected as a free gift, just included as a complimentary extra. This impressed me more than the free ream of paper did, because I had been expecting that. I hadn't expected the throat sweets and, even though I was fortunate enough not to have the flu, there must have been many other customers who were delighted to receive them and probably put them to good use straight away!

This is a brilliant example of customer excellence. The stationery supplier had probably negotiated a good price for buying in these throat sweets in bulk, and then instructed their 'pick and pack' staff to drop a pack into every order that was being dispatched to their customers that month. All it needed was a good idea. The additional cost per order was just pennies but the value added must have been immense. I'm sure that I wasn't the only recipient who told others about it and it certainly assured my loyalty as their customer.

I should add that I never opened my pack of throat sweets. Instead, I have used them many, many times as a prop when I have been running customer care courses as an illustration of customer excellence in action. I still have them, and I notice that the expiry date is 1998 – so for this particular stationery supplier the return on their investment has been truly immeasurable. That's the value of just one good idea.

Exercise

Have you ever been the recipient of customer excellence – where, as a customer, your expectations were significantly exceeded? If so, jot down the key points below.

....

....

....

Customer excellence is showing that you care

The following is another example of customer excellence, as described by the manager of a casino based on the south coast of England:

Excellent customer service is paramount in everything we do and we are always looking at ways of improving what we do. This is done through customer feedback forms, which are given out at the casino, and the customer then goes online to answer some questions about their casino experience.

A couple of ways we have exceeded customer expectations are as follows.

A couple, who were regular customers of the casino, moved away but still visited the area regularly. When they were due to come back about six months ago, they couldn't find a hotel room for the three weeks they were here. As they visit us regularly, we decided to arrange and pay for their stay in a local hotel ourselves. The couple in question were overjoyed and couldn't thank us enough.

Another example of us going that extra mile is that if one of our regular customers is ill or in hospital, we always send them flowers as a way of saying that we are thinking of them. Also, anyone who visits us on their birthday is given a free drink and a small gift as our way of saying happy birthday.

I would add that this particular casino has a large bar/restaurant area in which regular events, such as business networking lunches, are hosted. When I attended a lunch there recently, it transpired that over the last 11 months the casino had been holding fundraising events for a local cancer relief charity and in that time had raised a total of £280,000. This clearly demonstrates a caring culture and, in addition to the examples already mentioned, shows that they really value their customers.

Also notice that they actively use customer feedback as a tool for thinking up new initiatives and responding positively to customers' wants, needs and ideas for improvements.

Think about the customer experience

The following is the story of how Waterstones bookshops originated, based on a desire to enhance the customer experience of browsing and buying books.

Following redundancy, Tim Waterstone opened his first bookshop in 1982 on Old Brompton Road, London. At the time, he had only £6000 of his own money, but managed to raise the rest of the £100,000 he needed to get started. His intention was to build a chain of bookshops with a wide specialist range, a friendly atmosphere in which to browse and with knowledgeable staff on hand for advice. At that time, this was not how high street bookshops and newsagents operated, so his concept was quite different to the 'norm'. However, his ideas proved to be popular and, before long, Waterstones developed into a chain of bookshops throughout the UK.

What is particularly interesting is that at that time publishers were protected by the net book agreement, which meant that retailers of books were prevented from offering discounts on them. So Waterstones were selling the same products at exactly the same price as their competitors. In order to succeed, Tim Waterstone chose to step into his customers' shoes and focus on the whole experience of browsing and buying books in his stores. What would make the experience more enjoyable? What would make the customer want to come back and do it again? And what would encourage the customer to recommend the Waterstones experience to others?

The following are some of the features that contributed to the success of Waterstones. Although they probably sound quite commonplace now, back in the 1980s these things were different enough to make the difference:

- **Books put out on display on tables**. Generally, bookshops displayed their wares only on shelves, with their window displays featuring new publications. However, if a potential customer is browsing rather than looking for a specific book, their attention will be drawn to the books lying on a table. Rather like visiting someone in their home, if there are books or magazines lying on a coffee table, very soon your eyes will be drawn to them, probably out of curiosity.
- **Comfortable seating for customers**. Browsing while standing gets uncomfortable after a while, and if that element of discomfort kicks in before a desirable book has been discovered then the potential customer will probably leave without making a purchase. Where space allowed, squashy armchairs and other forms of seating were installed in Waterstones shops so that browsers could relax and take their time to review any books that interested them.

- **Knowledgeable staff**. I was fortunate enough to be seated next to Tim Waterstone at a business networking event several years ago. We had a fascinating discussion, during which he told me that many of his staff were themselves aspiring authors. This meant that, for them, working in an environment of books and literature was like living the dream. Staff were encouraged to select and review books themselves and to write a personal recommendation on a small piece of paper and attach it to the shelf where the book was stocked. Anyone curious to know more about the book could then speak to the member of staff who had written the recommendation. Many of Waterstones, staff have indeed gone on to become successful authors, including the following:
  - David Mitchell (*Cloud Atlas*)
  - Anna Dale (*Dawn Undercover* and *Whispering to Witches*)
  - Stuart Hill (*Cry of the Icemark* and *Blade of Fire*)
  - Alan Bissett (*The Incredible Adam Spark*)
  - Jeff Noon (*Vurt*)
  - Sonia Overall (*A Likeness*)
  - Oliver Jeffers (*Lost and Found*)
- **Coffee shops**. Again, space permitting, coffee shops with seating are included in the Waterstones experience. This has the added advantage of also attracting in passers-by who pop in for a coffee and then tempting to browse some books while they are there.

- **Events**. Starting in a small way in the early days with storytelling sessions for children, in 2007 Waterstones shops held over 5000 events and activities. When a Harry Potter book was published in July of that year, around 250,000 people attended their midnight openings around the UK, Ireland and Europe. Branches throughout the UK regularly host book signings and stand-up shows featuring a wide range of celebrities. And Waterstones is also associated with 15 literary festivals, including the Cheltenham Literary Festival and the Bath Children's Literary Festival.
- **Spotting new market trends**. Tim Waterstone, who is himself a published author, anticipated a demand for books by writers who were just emerging in the 1980s, such as Salman Rushdie, Ian McEwan, John Banville and Martin Amis. By embracing this new, developing market, Waterstones shops were positioned as being a little different to other mainstream high street booksellers.

In more recent years, Waterstones has embraced online book sales, issued loyalty cards to its customers and gained a reputation for occupying buildings of architectural or historical interest while retaining their original character and features. Examples include the Piccadilly (London) branch, which used to be Simpsons of Piccadilly, a department store that originally opened in 1936. During the early 1950s, scriptwriter Jeremy Lloyd was employed as a junior assistant at Simpsons; he drew on his experiences to come up with the idea for the highly popular 1970s/80s television sitcom *Are You Being served?*.

In the basement of Waterstones in Canterbury, and on display, are the remains of a Roman bath-house floor – a scheduled ancient monument. In the same building is a 21-year-old escalator, which the repair company believes may possibly be the oldest working escalator between London and Paris.

So, having set up Waterstones for £100,000 in 1982, Tim Waterstone sold it to WH Smith in 1993 for £47 million. Since then, it has been bought and sold a couple more times and, even though the book retailing industry has been impacted by the rise in popularity of e-books and e-book readers such as the Kindle, Waterstone's remains a popular, respected high street presence. In 2006, in a BrandIndex survey, Waterstone's came top of the high street retailers for service, quality, satisfaction and corporate reputation.

In an earlier chapter, we looked at mission statements. Tim Waterstone has been quoted as saying that mission statements are no good if customers can't understand them and staff can't buy into them. The following is Waterstones' mission:

> *To be the leading bookseller on the high street and online, providing customers with the widest choice, great value and expert advice from a team passionate about bookselling. Waterstones aims to interest and excite its customers and continually inspire people to read and engage in books.*

Ideas for achieving customer excellence

Remember that the key concept of customer excellence is to consistently exceed your customers' expectations. This need not require a large financial investment, but it does require an investment of your thoughts and ideas.

Let's recap on the initiatives used by the organizations featured in this chapter:

- **Topical or seasonal add-ons**. The stationery supplier that was sending out free medicated throat sweets during a bout of influenza. When a customer receives something that is immediately helpful to them, and which they weren't expecting, they will attach great value to it. I know of accountants who email their clients the day after a budget has been announced, explaining exactly what all the changes mean in 'real language' instead of political speak.

What could you give to your clients that would be valued?

....

....

....

- **Showing that you care**. The casino that sends flowers to customers who are ill or in hospital, and gives them a free drink and small gift to celebrate their birthday. I have met independent financial advisors who make a point of sending out birthday cards to all their clients. This activity doesn't cost a huge amount of money but is very much appreciated by the recipients and is more personal than just sending out Christmas cards.

How can you demonstrate to your customers that you care?

....

....

....

- **Enhancing the customer experience**. When you can't compete on product quality and price because they are fixed variables, as in the early days of Waterstone's, then you need to make the overall experience of buying from you more enticing. Step into the shoes of your typical customer and 'walk through' the buying process, at every stage being aware of their expectations and asking yourself how you can exceed them.

How can you enhance the customer's experience of dealing with you?

....

....

....

● **Product display**. However you showcase your products or services, it must be visually appealing. Think about refreshing any physical displays to make them more eye-catching. If customers visit your premises, ensure that cleanliness is a high priority. If you sell through a website, cast a critical eye over the ease of navigation and visual appeal of the relevant pages.

How can you make your products more appealing to your customers?

....
....
....

● **Physical comfort**. Depending on the nature of your business, your customers may visit you and may need to be provided with seating, perhaps in a reception area. A stained, uncomfortable, 'seen better days' sofa or chair sends out a message to your customers that you really don't care about them. Well-thumbed, months out of date magazines lying in an untidy heap on a coffee table don't help. Neither does the sight of used coffee cups that haven't been cleared away.

If you have a reception area, how can you improve the experience of spending time there?

....
....
....

Knowledgeable staff. When dealing with customer-facing staff, there is only one thing worse than hearing the words 'I don't know' in response to a question – being told the wrong information. You need to ensure not only that everyone in your organization receives the training that they need to do their jobs, but also that they are kept informed of any new products or services introduced, new procedures, or changes to existing ones. Communication starts at the top and it is essential that it cascades throughout all levels of staff. Anything less than that and you are doing your customers a great disservice.

How can training and knowledge sharing be improved in your business?

....

....

....

● **Refreshments**. In recent years, vending machines for customers' use have become more of a regular feature in businesses. Even department stores now have water coolers on the shop floor – retail therapy is thirsty work, after all! If you have a reception area, then at the very least you need to have a water cooler, if not a hot drinks vending machine as well. (Ensure that you also include a bin for the disposal of used plastic cups.) If your organization is an office environment with a staffed reception, then ensure that your reception staff offer a cup of tea or coffee to anyone who is likely to be kept waiting for ten minutes or more.

Do your customers have easy access to drinking water or hot drinks?

....

If not, what changes could you make to incorporate this facility?

....

....

....

● **Events**. This is an area where customer care and public relations can become very closely aligned. The casino mentioned earlier in this chapter was supporting a nominated charity for cancer relief. In holding fundraising events, they were not only helping the charity, but also promoting the casino as a venue to potential new customers who had never visited before. The activity also sent out a message that this was a caring business that chose to invest time and money to help people with serious illnesses.

Does your organization hold events? If not, how could this become a regular feature?

....
....
....

● **Spotting new market trends**. What are other businesses doing to look after their customers? It's always a good idea to be constantly vigilant, and not just by keeping an eye on other businesses in your industry. Novel and effective customer care initiatives that work in other industries may well work in yours too. Think about loyalty cards, newsletters and vouchers.

What customer care initiatives could you introduce that would differentiate you from your competitors?

....
....
....

Summary

In this chapter, we have explored the concept of achieving customer excellence by consistently exceeding the customer's expectations. The main benefits to be gained by doing this are:

- customer loyalty

- your customers become 'raving fans' and tell others about you, and your sales increase

- you build a reputation for yourself of being an organization that excels.

To illustrate this 'above and beyond' approach, examples included in this chapter spanned a variety of businesses, from a stationery supplier to a casino, with the main case study being Waterstone's bookshops.

Also reiterated in this chapter is the close relationship between customer care, marketing and public relations functions. The more effective you become at customer care, and particularly customer excellence, the more your customers will fulfil your marketing and public relations activities for you!

And, perhaps the best part – achieving customer excellence needs only a good idea; for example, the stationery supplier who decided to send out medicated throat sweets during an influenza epidemic. Someone in that organization came up with a good idea that would cost only a minimal amount, it was taken seriously, implemented and raving fans were created overnight!

In your organization, who is responsible for coming up with ideas for customer care initiatives? The answer is – everyone. Do you have a suggestion scheme in place? If not, think seriously about creating one. *Anyone* in your business might be sitting on the best idea that you've never had. Encourage them to put it forward, and be prepared to reward them for doing so.

SUNDAY MONDAY TUESDAY WEDNESDAY THURSDAY FRIDAY SATURDAY

Fact-check (answers at the back)

1. In order to achieve customer excellence:
   a) Over-promise and under-deliver ❏
   b) Meet customer expectations and nothing more ❏
   c) Under-promise and under-deliver ❏
   d) Consistently exceed customer expectations ❏

2. Which statement is true?
   a) Achieving customer excellence is expensive. ❏
   b) Just one good idea can generate customer excellence. ❏
   c) Customer excellence is a one-off activity. ❏
   d) Customer excellence is impossible to achieve. ❏

3. Which statement is true?
   a) Small, thoughtful actions can make a big impression. ❏
   b) A customer will notice only major initiatives. ❏
   c) There is little point in sending birthday cards to customers. ❏
   d) Customer feedback should not be used for generating new ideas. ❏

4. Waterstone's bookshops were founded by:
   a) Tom Waterstone ❏
   b) Jim Waterstone ❏
   c) Tim Waterstone ❏
   d) WH Smith ❏

5. Which statement is true?
   a) Books for sale should be displayed only on shelves. ❏
   b) A table display attracts visual attention. ❏
   c) People should always stand up to browse books. ❏
   d) Seating customers is a waste of space. ❏

6. Which statement is true?
   a) As long as staff know how to work a cash register, they are knowledgeable enough. ❏
   b) Customers shouldn't expect staff to have product knowledge. ❏
   c) A little knowledge is a dangerous thing; better to have none at all. ❏
   d) It is important for staff to be knowledgeable about the products and services offered by their organization. ❏

7. Which statement is true?
   a) Loyalty cards and vouchers are valued by customers. ❏
   b) Customers do not need to feel valued. ❏
   c) There is no such thing as a customer who is a 'raving fan'. ❏
   d) Marketing and public relations have nothing to do with customer care. ❏

8. Which statement is true?
a) Events are for staff only, not customers. ☐
b) Hosting events for the benefit of customers builds loyalty and a good reputation. ☐
c) Events are a costly overhead, and therefore are not feasible. ☐
d) An event will be supported only if a top celebrity attends. ☐

9. Which statement is true?
a) Customers don't notice whether products are displayed well or not. ☐
b) As long as your business premises are cleared once a week, they are clean enough. ☐
c) Your website is also your shop window and needs to be visually appealing. ☐
d) There is no need to provide water coolers or vending machines for use by customers. ☐

10. Which statement is true?
a) The 'customer experience' has nothing to do with you; it's all in their mind. ☐
b) Customers will always buy the cheapest product or service available. ☐
c) Your reception area is a great place to dump very old magazines. ☐
d) Customer care initiatives being used in other industries may well work in your business too. ☐

THURSDAY

Excellence in
communication

You cannot not communicate. Even if you are not speaking out loud, your body language is 'speaking' for you. The clothes you are wearing convey a message which will either enhance your degree of professionalism or detract from it. If you are wearing an overpowering perfume or cologne or, even worse, have a strong, unpleasant body odour, you have communicated a negative message to your customers and they may well decide that they don't want to interact with you and take their business elsewhere.

In this chapter, we will explore all aspects of communication, whether face to face, over the telephone or in writing. Using proven, effective NLP (Neuro Linguistic Programming) techniques, you will learn how to build rapport easily, effortlessly and rapidly. You will understand what makes everyone different and unique, and therefore why it is essential to have flexibility in your communication style.

You will also learn how to calm down an angry customer, easily and assertively, without getting sucked into their emotional state. You will discover the language to use and the actions to take to generate the best possible outcomes, which could even result in your most challenging customer becoming your biggest fan.

And, if you are an aspiring author, then there is a real gem in this chapter for you. I will share with you a technique that JK Rowling uses in every Harry Potter book to build rapport with her readers through the written word. So, if you're sitting comfortably, let's begin . . .

What makes everyone different and unique?

Each one of us is as individual as a fingerprint. We might be similar to others; however, there will always be differences that set us apart. The way that we process information, think, feel and behave creates our uniqueness, which influences the way that we communicate with others and how we like others to communicate with us.

The following diagram illustrates how we take in information (external events), pass it through our own individual set of 'filters', make sense of it, react to it emotionally and physically and, finally, behave in a way that feels appropriate to us.

Let's explore this in more detail.

The only way that we can take in the world that is going on around us is through our five senses. However, if we tried to absorb *everything* that is going on around us all the time, it would be more than our conscious minds can handle. Your conscious mind can process only seven plus or minus two things at a time; in other words, a maximum of nine things. Any more than that, and it will get overloaded and forget or overlook things. However, your unconscious mind makes two million neural connections a second; this is your 'power house'. When you hear it said that we use only five per cent of our brains, it is a reference to the very limited conscious mind. The remaining 95 per cent is our unconscious mind.

To protect the conscious mind from overload, everyone has a set of 'filters', made up of such things as memories, decisions, values, beliefs, attitudes, language and much more. These filters are created by our experiences as we progress through life, and because everyone's experience of life is different, everyone's filters are unique.

The role of the filters is to delete, distort or generalize information coming in, in order to make sense of it. The information then becomes an 'internal representation' – in other words, it is re-presented internally as a thought. Attached to the thought is a state of mind, so it may be a happy thought, a sad thought, an angry thought and so on. And allied to the state of mind is the physiology, or body language.

The connection between thought, state and physiology is a powerful one and we can test it out here.

Exercise

Sit up straight in your chair, look up at the ceiling, hold a big smile on your face and try to feel really miserable. Really try hard now.

You may have found that difficult, so now try the opposite. Slump down in your chair, look down at the ground, hold a miserable expression on your face and try to feel really happy.

What you may have discovered for yourself is that the mind and body are very much linked. All that occurred during that exercise was that you adopted two quite different types of body language, yet you may have found that it was difficult, perhaps even impossible, to experience a state of mind that was incongruent with your physiology.

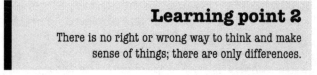

Learning point 1

The fastest way to change your state of mind is to change your body language.

Back to the diagram. The output from the information processing that goes on in your mind is your behaviour. This is your reaction to the 'external event' that you have just experienced, according to how your filters interpreted it. In your mind, you carry your own unique 'map of the world' and you use it to make sense of the 'territory' out there. This process determines how you conduct yourself at all times and it will always feel right for you. Somebody else in identical circumstances might behave differently in accordance with their unique set of filters, and that will be right for him or her, although it might appear to be completely wrong to you.

Learning point 2

There is no right or wrong way to think and make sense of things; there are only differences.

So how does this fit into customer care? Let's suppose your customer has at some time in the past had a bad experience with a product or service similar to the one they have purchased from you. Perhaps they tried to complain in order to get the fault corrected and were met with an extremely negative, unhelpful response. Maybe this caused them to lose money – it certainly made them very angry.

Now they have become your customer and a slight problem has arisen with the product or service you have supplied. Because they stored some very negative memories as a result of the past bad experience, these may now come to the surface and influence the way they behave towards you. To you, the customer seems to be over-reacting to a minor problem. You feel their behaviour is inappropriate and, being on the receiving end, you are now becoming defensive and perhaps even angry. If you continue in this vein, not only will you probably lose this customer, and possibly your temper, but you will reinforce their now very negative perception of your organization and your industry.

There is a saying, often attributed to Eleanor Roosevelt: 'No-one upsets me unless I allow it.' No matter how someone is behaving towards you, they cannot make you feel anything that you haven't chosen to feel. It may have been an unconscious choice on your part, but, nevertheless, it *was* your choice.

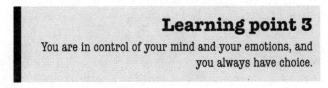

Learning point 3

You are in control of your mind and your emotions, and you always have choice.

So, given that everyone is different and unique, we need to find a way to 'build a bridge' across to their personal model of the world. We do this through building rapport.

Rapport

What is rapport? It is a term used to describe how two or more people feel *in sync* or *on the same wavelength* because they feel alike. It stems from an old French verb, *'rapporter'*, which means, literally, to carry something back. In the sense of how people relate to each other, it means that what one person sends out, the other sends back. For example, they may realize that they share similar values, beliefs, knowledge or behaviours around common interests.

Rapport embodies empathy; it is a two-way connection and is, in effect, the bridge across from my model of the world to yours. Having rapport with someone nurtures a better understanding, leading to a greater spirit of mutual co-operation. Resistance or negativity in a customer may indicate that rapport is missing.

Rapport builds naturally and can often be witnessed when the body language of two people interacting with each other ends up matched or mirrored. Be clear on the difference between these two: matching means identical, i.e. both people have their right leg crossed over their left and are leaning to their left, whereas mirroring means that one person is the mirror image of the other. So, if one has his right leg crossed over his left and is leaning to his left, the other person will have her left leg crossed over her right and be leaning to her right. You are more likely to end up *matched* with someone you are sitting or standing next to and *mirrored* with someone opposite you. Both are external indicators that rapport has been built.

It is of course possible to hasten along the process of rapport building by deliberately matching or mirroring the other person. If you choose to do this, subtlety is essential! If what you are doing is too obvious, it can cause offence.

The following diagram is a pie chart showing the three elements of communication – physiology (body language),

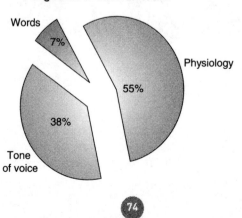

Segments of communication

tone of voice and words – and their relative proportions. Much research has been conducted on these figures, principally by Professor Emeritus of Psychology, Albert Mehrabian.

As you can see, the largest element in communication is physiology. Remember that you can't not communicate; your body language speaks for you, even before you've opened your mouth and uttered a single word. However, on the telephone, you have lost this largest piece of the pie; your body language cannot be seen, although a smile can be heard. When you speak with a smile, your voice sounds happier and more positive, so it's always a good idea to answer the phone with a smile on your face.

Let's look at each of these components in turn, to explore how you can utilize them to build rapport.

Physiology (55 per cent)

Matching or mirroring the other person's posture, gestures and movements, *with subtlety*, is the first place to start. Be very careful to avoid mimicry if, for example, they use very expansive arm gestures when they speak. If you suddenly start doing the same when this is not your normal behaviour, you may cause offence. Instead, use similar gestures on a smaller scale, i.e. hand movements rather than arm movements.

Match the breathing rate. When two people laugh together, their breathing is matched and if you're laughing with someone, you probably have a good rapport with them. Watch for the rise and fall of the shoulders and upper chest area, and match your breathing to theirs. If you are a man matching with a woman, be very careful that your eyes do not stray lower than shoulder level. It's no good excusing yourself by saying 'but I was just watching your breathing rate'; you won't get away with it and you may well get a slap round the face!

Let's imagine for a moment that you have an angry customer in front of you. What has happened to their breathing rate? It has probably speeded up because, as we know, emotional state has an effect on physiology. Perhaps you've been in this situation; you chose to stay really calm and your customer, instead of calming down, got even angrier. The reason for this is that rapport was lacking. Your customer's unconscious mind was telling him or her that because you were so different to them, clearly you just didn't understand the gravity of the situation and so they would have to ramp up their own behaviour in order to make their point more clearly.

In this scenario, you can use a technique called *pacing and leading*. If, while you are listening to your angry customer, you match their rapid breathing rate, you are expressing empathy and building a bridge across to their model of the world. This is called *pacing*. After a minute or so of doing this, start to slow down your breathing rate. If sufficient rapport has been built, they will now start to follow you and slow down their breathing, which in turn will move them towards a calmer state. You are now *leading*. This is a very effective strategy and because the other person is responding at an unconscious level, it will feel completely natural to them and not manipulative at all. Remember that matched breathing is something that occurs naturally; you are just hastening that process along to help your customer feel that you really do understand their grievance.

The final thing that you can match on body language is the blink rate. Be very careful if the other person has a squint, so as not to cause offence; however, this is another very effective way of creating a similarity and building rapport.

Tone of voice (38 per cent)

Have you ever been speaking with someone who has a very strong accent or dialect, and you unwittingly picked it up and started reflecting it back to them? This is a guaranteed way of offending through mimicry, caused by your unconscious mind's desire to create a similarity and build rapport. This is more likely to happen during a telephone conversation, when physiology plays very little part and tone of voice becomes approximately 80 per cent of the communication.

Instead, you can match the following elements of the other person's voice:

- volume
- speed
- tone
- energy
- intonation
- phrasing.

Pacing and leading can also play a part in calming down an angry customer over the telephone, without taking on board their angry emotional state. By sounding like them, even temporarily, they feel understood and it then becomes much easier for you to deal with their problem.

Exercise

In a very calm, quiet voice, read the following out loud:

'I cannot believe you've had this trouble, Mr Jones. This isn't like us at all. Now what I'm going to do is to make a note of everything you've told me, investigate it all personally and come back to you with an answer by the end of today. Is that acceptable to you?'

If you were saying this to a receptive, albeit angry, customer, they might let you get to the end of it without interrupting. However, there is a 50 per cent chance that they would jump in after the second sentence and start ranting again because there is a mismatch between your tone of voice and theirs.

So now read out the section in quotes again and this time, for the first two sentences, speak a little more loudly and faster. Then continue by gradually slowing down your speed and turning down the volume until you speak the final sentence in a calm voice.

This time, you have matched your angry customer's tone of voice. They feel understood and so are now prepared to enter into a calmer conversation with you. All you did was increase your energy levels for the first two sentences – and you didn't have to get angry to do that. The words you used were exactly the same both times – only the sound of your voice was different.

Words (seven per cent)

This is the smallest component of communication, but over the telephone it increases in value to about 20 per cent. In terms of matching, listen for the following:

● *Key words* – these are either individual words or short phrases that we like and use a lot. They vary from person to person and may include words such as:
   – basically
   – actually
   – cool
   – you know
   – okay
   – at the end of the day.

If you hear someone using any word or short phrase repeatedly, then you are hearing their key words. When you respond to them, incorporate those same words into your reply, and you are then 'speaking their language'.

● *VHF words* – when we speak, we tend to use words that fit into our preferred 'channel' of communication. These can be:
  - *visual* – examples are 'I see what you mean', 'Looks good to me', 'Show me more', etc.
  - *hearing* – examples are 'I hear what you're saying', 'That rings a bell', 'Sounds familiar', etc.
  - *feeling* – examples are 'I want to get a grip on this idea', 'I'm going with my gut feeling', 'That really touched me', etc.

If you can hear someone using vocabulary that falls predominantly into one of these three channels, then adjust your language so that you are using the same type of words. When you do this, you have 'tuned into their wavelength'.

Rapport in writing

If you are writing to someone and you don't know their preferred VHF channel, or if you are writing promotional material which will be read by many people, then balance the number of VHF words that you use. This will ensure that at least one-third of your text will be tuning into your reader's wavelength.

For example, 'We *see* from our records that it is some time since we have *spoken* and *felt* this was a good time to write to you.'

And JK Rowling? Open any Harry Potter book at any page and you will see that she uses a good balance of VHF words on every page. No wonder her books are so hard to put down . . .

Summary

In this chapter, we have explored the concept of everyone being different and unique, determined by our unique sets of internal 'filters', which in turn influence how we make sense of things and react to them. Perhaps you have watched a film with a friend; you thought it was brilliant and he or she thought it was rubbish. Neither of you is right or wrong – you are both evaluating the film using your own sets of filters, which are different.

We all create our own private 'model of the world' that enables us to make sense of what is going on around us and drives our behaviour. Past experiences play a huge part in the creation of our model and can mean that someone else's behaviour seems inappropriate to us, whereas it feels 'right' to them.

Rapport is the key to effective communication and enables us to build a bridge across into someone else's model of the world. By using the principles of matching and mirroring body language, tone of voice and words, we can replicate natural rapport building in a fraction of the 'normal' time.

Remember that it is impossible to not communicate. This means that everything covered in this chapter can be put into practice any time, anywhere, with anybody. Communication is the most essential skill you have in your 'toolbox' – use it well and it will reward you amply.

SUNDAY MONDAY TUESDAY WEDNESDAY THURSDAY FRIDAY SATURDAY

Fact-check (answers at the back)

1. Which statement is true?
a) The conscious mind can process a minimum of 15 things at a time. ❏
b) The unconscious mind makes two million neural connections a second. ❏
c) The conscious mind is the 95 per cent of the brain that we use most. ❏
d) Your 'power house' is your conscious mind. ❏

2. Filters . . .
a) Are identical for everyone ❏
b) Remain exactly the same throughout life ❏
c) Can cause the conscious mind to become overloaded ❏
d) Make sense of incoming information ❏

3. Which statement is true?
a) The fastest way to change how you feel is to eat chocolate. ❏
b) Body language has nothing to do with feelings. ❏
c) Changing your physiology instantly changes your state of mind. ❏
d) Thoughts and emotions are completely disconnected. ❏

4. In your mind, you carry your unique:
a) Model of the world ❏
b) Telephone directory ❏
c) Map of the London underground ❏
d) European road atlas ❏

5. Which statement is true?
a) Matching and mirroring are not natural processes. ❏
b) 'Rapport' comes from an old Italian verb. ❏
c) When deliberately matching someone else, movements should be exaggerated. ❏
d) Rapport enables a bridge to be built across to someone else's model of the world. ❏

6. The three elements of communication are:
a) Physiology, tone of voice, words ❏
b) Eye contact, handshake, written word ❏
c) Dress code, smiling, gestures ❏
d) Telephone, face to face, email ❏

7. Which statement is true?
a) Physiology is 58 per cent of communication. ❏
b) Words make up the smallest element of communication. ❏
c) Tone of voice is worth 70 per cent over the telephone. ❏
d) Spacing and leading is a rapport-building technique. ❏

8. Which statement is true?
a) Mimicking an accent builds rapport rapidly. ☐
b) Breathing is mismatched when people laugh together. ☐
c) Pacing and leading can help to calm down an angry customer. ☐
d) Matching somebody's blink rate serves no purpose. ☐

9. Which statement is true?
a) To 'speak somebody's language', match their key words. ☐
b) Until you speak, you are not communicating. ☐
c) If someone is quietly spoken, it's good to speak louder. ☐
d) It is impossible to build rapport over the telephone. ☐

10. Which statement is true?
a) 'I get the picture' indicates the hearing channel of communication. ☐
b) VHF stands for virtual, hearing, feeling. ☐
c) 'Feeling' people use words such as 'Tell me more'. ☐
d) To establish rapport in writing, use a balanced selection of VHF words. ☐

FRIDAY

Attitude is everything

In the last chapter, the point was made that it is impossible not to communicate. Even if you are not speaking, your body language speaks for you, and, in so doing, it conveys your state of mind. If a member of your customer-facing staff is feeling demotivated, not enjoying his or her job or even just having a 'bad hair day', his or her body language and general behaviour will reflect this. This means that there is a very strong chance that your customers will pick up on your staff member's negative attitude and this will damage their experience of doing business with you.

The definition of 'living the dream' in terms of a career is when your vocation is also your vacation. In other words, you love doing the work that you are employed to do and even if you weren't being paid to do it, you would still choose to do it anyway. Employees who are like this are totally self-motivated. They are natural peak performers and if every member of your staff is this type of person, then your organization is truly living the dream.

Probably, this is not quite the reality for you. So, in this chapter, we will explore attitude, motivation and how to positively enjoy being of service to customers.

When the customer is an inconvenience

Can you remember a time when, as a customer, you found yourself on the receiving end of somebody else's indifference, negativity even. Perhaps you dared to complain about a product or service and you were met with a hostile response, which was completely inappropriate. That may well have been the last time you dealt with that organization and, possibly, you warned others to avoid it too.

And yet, what you actually had was a bad experience with one individual, not with the whole organization. If you had been served by another member of staff, who was helpful, polite and genuinely interested in resolving your problem to the very best of their ability, your perception would have been completely different. You might even have ended up recommending that organization to your friends and family.

What this means is that every individual within an organization is, at any time, representative of that organization. If one of your customer-facing staff has a big argument with their partner before coming into work one morning, and carries that anger around with them all day, there is a strong chance that they will end up snapping at your customers. Anyone on the receiving end of this unjustified treatment may well form a negative impression of your entire organization. After all, if one of your staff behaves like that, perhaps they all do.

HAVE YOU TRIED STICKING PLASTER?

So how do you know how your staff behave towards customers? You may have personally witnessed their standard of service by being present when they were dealing with a customer, either face to face or over the telephone. However, their behaviour when there is nobody present to observe or supervise them may be quite different.

Mystery shopper

One very effective way of finding out exactly how your staff treat your customers is to carry out a mystery shopper exercise. This means that you, or someone appointed by you, adopts the role of a customer to ascertain how your staff behave in the following areas:

- dealing with telephone enquiries
- dealing with face-to-face enquiries
- selling goods or services
- ordering goods to be collected or delivered
- arranging delivery of goods'to a customer's premises
- ensuring that delivery of the correct goods is carried out on schedule
- dealing with the return of faulty or unwanted goods
- dealing with complaints (face to face and over the telephone)
- dealing with a 'difficult' person and
- any other areas relative to your business.

By now, you will have created service standards and procedures, and communicated these to your staff, so carrying out a mystery shopper exercise is the ideal opportunity to check how well they have been understood and implemented. The results may also highlight situations that your staff need to deal with which you had not anticipated, so this provides an opportunity to revise and improve your standards and procedures.

Before carrying out a mystery shopper exercise, create a checklist of all the aspects you would like to review. For a face-to-face exercise, these could include:

- time taken to acknowledge and greet you
- if there was a queue, how many people were in it?
- friendliness of the greeting

- attentiveness of listening
- accurate understanding of your needs
- appropriateness of response
- accuracy of information provided
- speed of service
- standard of personal appearance
- general demeanour of the staff member(s)
- cleanliness and tidiness of the premises.

For a telephone exercise, the following could also be included:

- time taken to answer the phone
- friendliness and clarity of the greeting
- ease of being connected to the appropriate person
- if put on hold, for how long?
- if a request for a call back was made, did it happen and how long did it take?

If you are conducting a mystery shopper exercise by telephone, it is a good idea to record the call. There are many ways to do this, one of which is to use Skype, a free, downloadable software package that enables calls to be made via the internet. You can either use a headset connected to a desktop computer or laptop or use the computer's speakers and plug in a microphone. There are recording options that work in conjunction with Skype and these will generate a sound file at the end of the call. These recordings can then be used in staff training sessions as both good and not so good examples of how to handle incoming calls from customers.

I once worked with an estate agency that used a selection of recorded mystery shopper calls as part of their induction training for new staff. I remember one in particular in which the phone could be heard persistently ringing before the receiver was eventually picked up and put straight back down again to disconnect the call. This happened three times before the mystery shopper gave up. It transpired that these calls had been made just after 9.00 a.m. on a Monday morning and when the particular member of staff was 'confronted' with the evidence and asked for an explanation, he replied, 'I'm not a morning person!'

SUNDAY
MONDAY
TUESDAY
WEDNESDAY
THURSDAY
FRIDAY
SATURDAY

Learning point 1

If you have any members of staff with an attitude like this, you need to know about it before your customers let you know by taking their business elsewhere.

The motivated individual

In an earlier chapter, Waterstone's featured as a case study in enhancing the 'customer experience'. Tim Waterstone personally recruited his first 500–600 staff and has been quoted as saying, 'A good attitude, good spirit and optimism in somebody is a precious thing. Without this, no matter how good somebody is technically, they'll bring you down.'

So motivation starts at the recruitment stage. Once employed, there needs to be a working environment that nurtures ongoing motivation for *all* staff. Research has shown that money (in terms of salary) is not the top motivator in the workplace. People need to feel acknowledged and valued for the job that they do and this can be achieved by verbal, genuine praise and awards, which may or may not be financial. In the world of cinema, an actor can be paid millions for appearing in a film and may receive great media reviews by critics, but what means the most to them is the ultimate accolade of being awarded an Oscar for their performance.

Motivation through employee involvement

A good example of an organization that fully involves its staff in its day-to-day operations and recognizes their contributions by awarding a performance-related bonus for everyone is the John Lewis Partnership.

Founded in 1864 by John Spedan Lewis, the company has a written constitution that sets out the principles, governance system and rules of the partnership. It states that the happiness of its members is the partnership's ultimate purpose, recognizing that such happiness depends on having a satisfying job in a successful business. It establishes a system of rights and responsibilities, which places on all partners the requirement to work for the improvement of the business in the knowledge that everyone shares the rewards of success.

This system works so well that in March 2011, the 76,500 staff, or 'partners', who co-own the retail group received a bonus of

18 per cent of their annual salary in that month's wages. It is considered that the motivation generated by employee ownership gives the company a competitive advantage, which helped to produce a 20 per cent increase in pre-tax profits over the previous year. The John Lewis Partnership also won 'Retailer of the Year' at the Oracle Retail Week Awards in 2011.

One of the methods used by the company to focus on the happiness of its members is the annual partner survey, which was first introduced in 2003. The survey is distributed to all partners and is anonymous, with each store receiving separate results so that concerns can be easily identified and acted upon without compromising that anonymity. Included in the survey are questions related to job satisfaction, pay, career development, management, their branch, the democratic bodies and the partnership as a business. Replies are processed by an external company so that no individual responses are seen by anyone in the partnership. In 2011, some 90 per cent of the partners took part in the survey, with the real value coming from the questions, discussions and actions prompted by the results.

As a democratic business, all major business decisions are shared with partners and active communication is nurtured through councils, forums and committees at local, divisional and partnership levels. There are also online communication channels and publications to keep partners fully informed of business developments. The company's weekly publication, The Gazette, was originally created by John Spedan Lewis to communicate news to partners and provide them with a forum for airing their views. It still serves the same purpose today, and partners can write in to The Gazette anonymously, if they wish, on any matter.

Considering that the John Lewis Partnership is a retail business that has flourished during an economic downturn that has hit many retail businesses hard, then staff attitude and motivation must be playing a major role in its success.

Employee engagement

Research has shown that the majority of employees would like to take on challenges and are prepared to put in the extra effort needed to excel in their work. However, the reality is that only a small minority actually do so. What this means is that most staff are performing well below their potential, which is known as the 'engagement gap'. Staff may physically be at work but they are not 'there' in any other sense. This is known as 'presenteeism', as opposed to 'absenteeism', when they don't even turn up at all.

Exercise

The following questions are designed to explore how well you know, develop, motivate, involve and reward your staff. The results will identify for you areas within your organization where improvements could be made.

● What does your organization do to build the kind of working relationships between managers and staff, such that staff feel they are 'known' and understood?

....

....

....

How does your organization measure staff morale and what actions are taken to address any morale issues?

....
....
....

How does your organization encourage staff to develop their skills and capabilities?

....
....
....

Does your organization have training programmes readily available (either in house or outsourced) and a budget to fund staff training and development?

....
....
....

Are staff recognized and rewarded for initiating their own development?

....
....
....

How well does your organization communicate its vision, mission and long-term goals?

....
....
....

Do staff fully understand how they fit into this 'big picture' and that everyone's job role plays an important part?

....
....
....

Are your directors seen to be ambassadors for fulfilling the organization's vision and mission, and how much do staff feel inspired by them?

....
....
....

What are the communication channels within your organization and how well is important information cascaded down from director level throughout the organization?

....
....
....

How well do different departments or functions interact with each other and are there any processes to encourage open communication/good working relationships between them?

....
....
....

How are people recognized and rewarded within your organization, such that they feel valued for their efforts?

....
....
....

Do your managers actively pursue a policy of 'catching them doing something right', praising in public and, if necessary, criticizing in private?

....
....
....

If you found yourself guessing at some of the answers related to how your staff feel, then you might like to consider carrying out an employee satisfaction survey. As with your customers, don't assume that no news is good news. Find out what's going on for your staff.

Is the glass half full or half empty?

Would you like the good news or the bad news? Here is the good news – optimism is contagious, and it can generate a fantastic, energized, friendly working environment where it is a joy to come into work.

Here is the bad news – pessimism is also contagious, and it can dampen anyone's enthusiasm, drain staff of their energy and even contribute to absenteeism. After all, who would look forward to spending their working day in an environment like that?

Your staff will also be positively or negatively influenced by the environment in which they work. This means that if they deal with customers, either face to face or over the telephone, their demeanour and attitude will determine their behaviour. The following is an example of a workplace where I cannot imagine any employee being able to feel miserable.

Fruit Towers

Innocent Drinks is a UK-based company founded in 1998 by three Cambridge graduates – Richard Reed, Adam Balon and Jon Wright. At the time, they were working in consulting and advertising; however, after spending six months working on recipes and £500 on fruit, they took a stall at a London music festival and sold their smoothies to the public. People were asked to deposit their empty bottles in a 'yes' or 'no' bin depending on whether they thought the three friends should quit their jobs to make smoothies full time. At the end of the festival, the 'yes' bin was full, with only three empty bottles in the 'no' bin. They went into work the next day and resigned, and Innocent Drinks was born. It now has a 75 per cent share of the £169 million UK smoothie market and the company sells two million smoothies a week.

The company's headquarters, Fruit Towers, has recently been relocated to another part of London in order to accommodate the growing staff head count. However, as with the original location, it has been furnished to promote the 'happy-go-lucky' image:

- Floors covered in artificial turf rather than carpets.
- Every office area has its own break-out space with soft seating, sofas and a small kitchen area.
- Picnic tables replace a cafeteria.
- An original red British phone box (in the office area).
- Banana-shaped telephones.
- A large lever with the instruction, 'Last leaver, pull the lever', which shuts down the power for the office at night.
- A green lamp that flashes when the outside temperature reaches a suitable level, prompting staff to open the windows as the air conditioning cuts out.
- Delivery vans, lined up outside the offices, are either covered in artificial turf or have been 'decorated' to look like cows.

Office tours take place regularly and members of the public are invited at random to attend the annual general meeting, which has been renamed 'A Grown-up Meeting'.

Add to this working environment the product, which is sugar free, healthy, tasty, consisting of whole fruit and vegetable products in minimal packaging, using 100 per cent recycled bottles, plus the fact that Innocent Drinks donates ten per cent of its profits to charities every year, and it's not difficult to find happy, motivated staff on board.

Summary

Some people are naturally cheerful and helpful, with a genuine desire to be of service to others. If you are able to recruit people like this into your customer service function, then you will have a force to be reckoned with!

Others need to have these attributes nurtured. They need to feel valued, and they need to be openly recognized for doing a good job. They need to know that their voice will be heard if they have a point to make. They need to feel fully involved in the day-to-day running of their organization and to know that their job role makes a worthwhile contribution.

The quality of the communication within your organization will have a powerful effect on the morale and motivation of staff at all levels. When staff feel they are being 'kept in the dark', they start to shut down. They will find it hard to 'go the extra mile' for an unappreciative employer and a negative attitude will soon be conveyed to your customers.

SUNDAY
MONDAY
TUESDAY
WEDNESDAY
THURSDAY
FRIDAY
SATURDAY

However, just as customer excellence can be achieved with a good idea, so can employee excellence. It really takes very little effort to put in place the kind of initiatives that can generate consistently positive attitudes from your staff. You don't have to rip up the carpet and replace it with artificial turf; all you have to do is communicate with your staff. Ask them what they think, how they feel and what ideas they have to improve the business. And then listen . . .

Fact-check (answers at the back)

1. An ideal career is when:
   a) Your day-to-day work is a chore ❏
   b) Your vocation is your vacation ❏
   c) Somebody else has chosen your career for you ❏
   d) Your work is just something that pays the bills ❏

2. Which statement is true?
   a) Natural peak performers are self-motivated. ❏
   b) Peak performer means 'mountaineer'. ❏
   c) Peak performers hate their jobs. ❏
   d) There is an age limit to being a peak performer. ❏

3. Which statement is true?
   a) It's acceptable to be indifferent to a complaining customer. ❏
   b) Only directors are representative of their organization. ❏
   c) Sales staff should not be expected to be representative of their organization. ❏
   d) Every individual within an organization is representative of that organization. ❏

4. Which statement is true?
   a) The only way to find out how your staff are performing is to install hidden cameras and microphones. ❏
   b) If your staff insist that they're doing a fantastic job, then clearly there is no room for improvement. ❏
   c) Using a mystery shopper is an effective way of stepping into your customer's shoes. ❏
   d) There is no need to have a checklist prepared before making a mystery shopper call. ❏

5. Which statement is true?
   a) Recorded mystery shopper calls can be used in staff training sessions. ❏
   b) Staff shouldn't be expected to be polite in the mornings if that is not their preferred time of day. ❏
   c) As long as there is music playing, it's acceptable to leave a caller on hold for any length of time. ❏
   d) A 'difficult' customer deserves a hostile response. ❏

6. Which statement is true?
a) A positive attitude will not be apparent in a candidate at a recruitment interview. ❏
b) Motivation starts at the recruitment stage. ❏
c) A self-motivated person will never 'go the extra mile' without being asked. ❏
d) An optimistic attitude is unrealistic and irritating. ❏

7. Which statement is true?
a) Salary is the top motivator in the workplace. ❏
b) Nobody needs to be acknowledged for doing a good job. ❏
c) Criticizing in public is a good idea. ❏
d) Verbal, genuine praise contributes to motivation. ❏

8. Which statement is true?
a) The John Lewis Partnership was founded in 1864. ❏
b) Only the directors are 'partners'. ❏
c) It is considered to be an autocratic business. ❏
d) 50 per cent of the partners took part in the 2011 survey. ❏

9. Which statement is true?
a) Information is power; therefore communication should be severely restricted. ❏
b) People appreciate being 'kept in the dark' as ignorance is bliss. ❏
c) Good communication at all levels in an organization helps staff to feel valued. ❏
d) Communication has nothing to do with staff motivation. ❏

10. Which statement is true?
a) Innocent Drinks sells half a million smoothies a week. ❏
b) Fruit Towers has artificial turf instead of carpets in the office areas. ❏
c) It's easy to feel miserable in a 'happy-go-lucky' work environment. ❏
d) Innocent's delivery vans are covered in cotton wool to look like sheep. ❏

SUNDAY

MONDAY

TUESDAY

WEDNESDAY

THURSDAY

FRIDAY

SATURDAY

SATURDAY

Plan to excel

This chapter will focus on helping you to become a recognized market leader in customer care by creating and maintaining a reputation that will speak for you. In the previous chapters, much of the groundwork has been done in giving you an awareness of all the different aspects that contribute to customer excellence. In this chapter, we will aim to consolidate all those aspects into defining a 'way forward' that will generate an ongoing momentum throughout your organization.

For some businesses, this 'way forward' might just be a matter of reinforcing existing processes and practices. For others, the introduction of new customer care techniques may generate a culture change – for the better, of course! The common denominator is one of communicating service standards, amended processes, new initiatives and so on to staff at all levels, using the most appropriate methods.

The key concept, which *must* be embraced for customer excellence to be achieved, is that leadership in customer care comes from the top. It is not just the responsibility of customer-facing staff; it is the responsibility of *everyone* within an organization. This means that training programmes and workshops are as relevant for company directors as they are for staff manning a help desk.

Also, your customers are not just external to your organization. You also have internal customers who need to be accorded an appropriate level of service without being constantly compromised in favour of fee-paying customers. Let's look at this area first.

Internal customers

Every function within an organization exists to play a part in the overall process of the organization's business transactions. The relationships between these different functions are co-dependent. Some of these relationships run smoothly, like a well-oiled machine. However, others sometimes break down, often resulting in fingers of blame being pointed in multiple directions.

It is at times like these that departments can end up behaving as if they are in competition with each other and, consequently, working relationships deteriorate. Any spirit of co-operation that was in place ceases and somewhere, at the far end of all this turmoil going on, is an external customer being let down.

Again, direction and leadership needs to come from the top. Even though every department is focused on achieving goals and targets within allocated budgets, everyone is working for the same organization. It can be very easy to lose sight of this bigger picture, and this is where leadership by example plays a key role.

It is important that staff at all levels in an organization have visibility of their directors 'walking the talk', that is living the vision and the mission and demonstrating that they are in touch with, and care about, everyone within the organization. If any new key clients or major orders have been won, then it's good to communicate this to all staff and congratulate them on the parts that they have played in this achievement.

It is also a good plan to encourage cross-functional communication, in order to engender a better understanding of how other functions operate, timescales they are subject to, challenges they regularly encounter, and the role they play in the whole scheme of things. This can be done, for example, by inviting someone from another department to come along and give a presentation at your next department meeting.

This is the type of information that needs to be included in induction training for new staff, and perhaps also documented in an employee manual. In a large organization, it is easy for individuals to feel that they are just a cog in a large wheel; however, wheels cannot turn without those cogs. Everyone needs to know how they fit into the organization, how important their working relationships with others are and how their individual job role contributes to the overall success of the organization.

In short, the organization that has staff who feel informed and valued will be perceived by customers as an organization with which they would like to do business. The organization that cares about its staff also cares about its customers, and this is a great culture to nurture.

Training

Induction training for new staff is essential, and your customer service standards and procedures can be included in this. However, training in customer care should not be seen as a one-off. Even staff who have been on the head count for a few years will benefit from 'refresher' training; after all, customer expectations are constantly changing, particularly with developing technology. Also, if the attendees on a course are a mixture of some who have been with the company for only a short time and others who have been employed for many years, the exchange of experiences and knowledge between them will be invaluable.

Similarly, if the course is deliberately positioned to be cross-functional, with attendees drawn from a variety of different departments, then they will not only learn about customer care, but they will also learn and understand more about each other.

Beware of having too many attendees on a training session. There is nothing worse than being faced with a group of people with their arms folded defiantly, sighing heavily, telling you in an angry tone of voice that they are only these because their managers sent them. It is better to opt for smaller groups and to make the training a 'workshop' in which ideas, opinions and other contributions are welcomed.

It is also important that people know why they are attending the workshop. There is nothing worse than being faced with a group of people with their arms folded and who are sighing heavily and tell you in an angry tone of voice that they are only there because their managers sent them. In this frame of mind, these people will be completely disconnected from the training; they will not be remotely interested in learning anything at all and they will resent the time they are having to spend away from their jobs.

Be aware that everyone's favourite radio station is WIIFM, or 'What's In It For Me?'. Think about how you can make the idea of attending a customer care workshop sound interesting and intriguing, exciting even. The following are some ideas that you could use.

- You are creating new customer service standards for the company and you are keen to get input from staff on their techniques for dealing with customers and their problems in order to get the best results. Everyone invited to attend will have the opportunity to review and comment on the new standards you are creating, as well as put forward their own ideas for 'best practice'. The best idea put forward at each workshop will win a prize (make this worth having, for example a £25 voucher for a retailer of their choice).
- The company is thinking of introducing incentives for outstanding customer service and everyone within the organization will be eligible, even those who do not deal directly with external customers. The workshop will be a vehicle for communicating the scheme to staff, gaining

their input and agreement to criteria being set for achieving an award (which could be financial or something else they would prefer) and generally help them on their way to winning an award for themselves.

● Create a 'branded' customer service programme, to be rolled out throughout your organization. Make it fun and funky, without losing the underlying purpose, and start promoting it well before the training workshops start, to generate curiosity and anticipation. For example, I once created a customer service programme for a client in the insurance industry and called it 'In Step'. The theme was all about being 'in step' with their customers, so it embraced rapport building on the telephone, listening skills, problem solving and so on. A logo for the programme was created, incorporating a couple of footprints, and posters were put up around the building along the lines of 'In Step – coming your way' and 'Are you In Step yet?' and so on. As part of the course content, I included a short session on line dancing! Part-way through the training day, we stopped and pushed all the tables and chairs back, I taught everyone a very simple line dancing routine and then everyone did it together to music. The whole point of line dancing is that everyone is 'in step' with each other, otherwise it doesn't work, so this made it relevant to the programme. Needless to say, everyone loved it: it was a great energizer and it made the programme memorable.

Note that if you choose to create a branded customer care programme and roll it out to your entire organization, this also generates a public relations opportunity. You can publicly announce that your organization cares so much about its customers that everyone, without exception, receives innovative training in being customer focused. However, be aware that this is a double-edged sword. Once you have gone public on this, customer expectations of service from your organization will increase, so staff must consistently put into practice what they have been taught.

Workshop content

In creating the content for a customer care workshop, think about including the following:

- **Objectives and outcomes for attendees** – people need to know why they are there and what they are going to get from it (WIIFM).
- **Definitions of all the elements that constitute customer care** – invite ideas from delegates as a brainstorming activity, ensuring that everything that needs to be identified does get identified. See Sunday's chapter for inspiration.

- **Examples of good and bad customer service** – this works well as an exercise. Divide into small groups and ask each group to come up with one example of outstandingly good customer service that they have received, and one example of extremely bad customer service. This often brings out some real horror stories, and also starts to get them into the idea of stepping into the shoes of the customer.
- **The expectations of your company's customers** – ask for their ideas, and then follow with the next question.
- **How well are you meeting their expectations?** Generally, delegates will believe that they are doing a good job of serving customers, so if you have any results from a customer satisfaction survey or from a mystery shopper exercise, this is a good time to present them.
- **Customer service standards** – these should encapsulate the principle of meeting customer expectations. In discussion with the group, check that the standards are seen as being realistic, to ensure that they are fully embraced by delegates.
- **Customer excellence** – leading on from just meeting service standards, this topic introduces the idea of going 'above and beyond' what the customer expects in order to achieve excellence. Relate it back to the earlier examples identified by the group of outstandingly good customer service.
- **How can we exceed customer expectations**? This encourages delegates to start identifying 'excellence initiatives'. The real bonus here is that because they are formulating these ideas themselves, any feasible ideas will automatically be fully supported by their 'authors'. Divide into small groups and ask each group to present three different ideas for achieving customer excellence. Among their answers there are bound to be some real 'gems' which could be implemented in your organization.
- **Rapport building** – this is an essential skill in customer service. You could include some of the tips and techniques explored in Thursday's chapter, 'Excellence in communication'.

- **Problem solving** – there are three golden rules that should always be observed when dealing with customers' problems, which are:

  1 **Always say what you can do rather than what you can't do** when resolving a customer problem. This will make you sound more positive and helpful, even if you are unable to provide the exact solution that the customer wants.

  2 **Always do what you say you will do**. It is essential to follow through on actions that you have promised a customer you will carry out. For example, if you have promised to ring them back by a certain time with an update, but at that time you have nothing new to tell them, ring them back anyway to tell them that. Don't leave them in the dark – they will assume that you don't care and you have abandoned them.

  3 **Take ownership of a customer's problem** if it is reported to you first. Even if it does require the involvement of another department to resolve it, monitor progress to ensure that it does get sorted out to the customer's satisfaction and within an acceptable timeframe.

- **Mystery shop other organizations in your industry**. This is an optional exercise that I have included in workshops in the past and which has worked particularly well. Here's what you do:

  1 Ask delegates to brainstorm all those elements that play a part in handling an incoming enquiry by telephone effectively, e.g. time taken to answer, friendliness of greeting, helpful attitude.

  2 List all of these on a flip chart and then ask delegates to prioritize them in order of importance to a potential customer.

  3 Divide into pairs and give each pair a pre-prepared list of four other organizations in your industry, with telephone numbers, and either provide them with a phone to make the calls or check that they are happy to use their own mobile phones. If necessary, lend them your mobile phone for the exercise.

  4 Using the prioritized list of elements to listen out for, each pair makes telephone enquiries to the organizations on their list and allocates marks out of ten against each of the elements.

5 Reconvene the whole group and take feedback. Check for any calls that were handled particularly well or particularly badly.

6 Bring out the learning point that they were speaking to just one individual within that organization. They could ring that same company again and speak to somebody else and have a completely different experience. Every individual is representative of their organization, and you never get a second chance to make a first impression.

Post training

It is important to keep the momentum of training going after the course is over. If you have incorporated this training into an induction programme, then providing your new starters with mentors for their first few months in the company is always a good idea.

If you have been encouraging staff to propose customer excellence initiatives during training, then it is to everyone's benefit to keep this ball rolling. Your organization may already have a 'suggestion scheme' in place, under which anyone can submit ideas for improvement and cost savings in any area of the organization. Think about expanding this to include customer excellence initiatives, with a prize for the best one submitted each month of, say, £100 in value.

The real bonus of this course of action is that it keeps everyone thinking about customer care all the time. It also means that your organization has developed into one that is serious about continuous improvement in your levels of customer service. And that is a very good reputation to have.

One good idea

The teabag was originally invented in 1908 when Thomas Sullivan, a New York tea and coffee merchant, started packaging loose tea in small hand-sewn silk bags as a convenient way to send tea samples to his customers. Recipients of these silk bags thought that the tea was intended to be brewed in the bags and so put these directly into their cups instead of removing the contents. As a result, the teabag was born.

Tetley Tea launched its teabag in Britain in 1953, which, like other tea companies' teabags, was the conventional square shape. However, someone came up with the idea of introducing round teabags and, in 1989, Tetley embarked on an advertising campaign promoting the benefits of the new shape. In a television advert, an animation demonstrated how tea leaves got caught up in the corners of a square tea bag, whereas in a round bag they could circulate freely and give the tea drinker an improved 'all-round flavour'.

Tetley's sales of the new round teabag went through the roof. Before long, its inventory turnover had increased by 30 per cent, and within 18 months it had gained brand leadership in the UK – all as a result of one good idea.

Internet customers

So far, we have focused on dealing with customers face to face or over the telephone; however, people are increasingly purchasing goods and services over the internet. The principles of customer care remain the same, in particular that if people are buying through your website, then they need to be able to contact customer support just as easily through your website.

The main challenge is that of managing customer expectations. If people are 'surfing the net' and making purchases in the early hours of the morning, they may expect that a complaint they have emailed to you will be answered more promptly than is realistic. This particularly applies to international customers, where there may be a time difference of several hours. The best way to handle this is for an automatic response to be sent out in reply to a customer's email, acknowledging receipt and providing a timescale within which the customer can expect to receive a personal reply. It is then essential that a customer support person responds to the individual within this time frame.

One of the major benefits of achieving customer excellence via the internet is that a delighted customer may give you a 'viral referral'; in other words, they sing your praises to friends and followers through a variety of social media sites.

There is, of course, a downside to this. A dissatisfied customer can also spread the word very quickly and very widely, which could seriously damage the reputation of your organization. Remember the iceberg model from Tuesday's chapter.

Your customer service standards should include a time frame within which complaints will be investigated and resolved. If a problem cannot be resolved within that time, then there needs to be regular communication with the customer to keep them up to date with progress. Although this applies to all your customers, it is imperative that this happens with your internet customers because these people are more likely to be users of Facebook, Twitter, LinkedIn and other social media sites.

Summary

In this final chapter, we have explored those things that need to happen to move your organization forward to becoming a recognized market leader in customer care. Training is a key element of this, and for *everyone* in an organization, not just those who deal directly with external customers. It is also important that a training programme addresses the 'What's in it for me?' question in order to gain the support of staff.

Once a training programme has kickstarted the customer excellence mentality, it is important to keep that momentum going with incentives and awards. A suggestion box might sound very basic, yet it is a practical way of encouraging people to put forward their ideas, with the assurance that they will be taken seriously and reviewed in a confidential environment. And a suggestion box doesn't need to be a physical box; it can be a virtual box with a dedicated email address.

We have also looked at the concept of internal customers and the benefits to the entire organization of improving cross-functional communication and understanding.

Leadership from the top and leadership by example are the real drivers for creating and sustaining customer excellence. However, the following two 'rules' also work very well:

The golden rule of customer care is to treat others as you would like to be treated.

The platinum rule of customer care is to treat others as they would like to be treated, and then some.

Fact-check (answers at the back)

1. Which statement is true?
   a) Customer care is purely the responsibility of customer-facing staff. ❏
   b) Leadership in customer care comes from the top. ❏
   c) Customer care is driven by your competitors. ❏
   d) Directors do not need training in customer care. ❏

2. Which statement is true?
   a) All customers are external to your organization. ❏
   b) Internal customers are other companies in your industry. ❏
   c) Internal customers are other departments in your organization. ❏
   d) Only external customers matter. ❏

3. Which statement is true?
   a) Directors need to be seen to 'walk the talk'. ❏
   b) Directors should be made to walk the plank. ❏
   c) Directors need to remain remote from their staff. ❏
   d) Only the sales force need to know about a major new order. ❏

4. Which statement is true?
   a) New starters should attend reduction training. ❏
   b) An induction course should not include any references to customer care. ❏
   c) Induction training is only necessary in large organizations. ❏
   d) Induction training is for new staff. ❏

5. Which statement is true?
   a) Customer care training needs to be recurring rather than a 'one-off'. ❏
   b) Customer expectations always remain the same. ❏
   c) If someone has been employed by the organization for five years, then there is nothing new they can learn about customer care. ❏
   d) Directors are exempt from customer care training. ❏

6. Which statement is true?
   a) 'Cross-functional' means that different functions get cross with each other. ❏
   b) Cross-functional training helps different departments understand each other. ❏
   c) There can never be too many attendees on a training course. ❏
   d) Delegates on a training course should all be from the same department. ❏

7. Which statement is true?
a) People don't need to know the reason they are attending a workshop. ❏
b) Everyone is comfortable to speak up in front of a large group of people. ❏
c) When attending a workshop, you must bring along a hammer and nails. ❏
d) Everyone's favourite radio station is WIIFM. ❏

8. Which statement is true?
a) A branded customer service programme can be rolled out throughout the organization. ❏
b) A good customer service programme is weird and meaningless. ❏
c) Incentives for delivering customer excellence are pointless. ❏
d) It is unlikely that any good ideas will come from staff on a workshop. ❏

9. Which statement is true?
a) Customers do not hold any expectations of service levels at all. ❏
b) Always tell a customer what you can't do for them. ❏
c) Always follow through and do what you say you will do. ❏
d) Never take ownership of a problem that isn't directly your fault. ❏

10. Which statement is true?
a) You should mystery shop only your own organization, not others. ❏
b) A suggestion scheme can help to maintain the momentum of training. ❏
c) Teabags have always been round in shape. ❏
d) Internet customers never shop outside of your working hours. ❏

Surviving in tough times

In tough economic times, when people are being careful about what they spend their money on, and indeed whether to spend it at all, the organizations that place great importance on the quality of their customer care are the ones that stand out from the rest. Your customers like to feel valued and appreciated, whether they are individuals or organizations. This book has covered a number of different aspects of customer care with an emphasis on aiming to achieve customer excellence, which can generate customer loyalty and referrals. The following ten tips are tried and tested ideas that can significantly raise your profile as an organization that really cares about its customers – every one of which is relatively inexpensive to implement.

1 Reward customer loyalty

When people are trying to be thrifty with their money, they love to receive vouchers and special offers. These could be in the form of, for example, money-off vouchers, buy one get one free vouchers or loyalty cards. Think about offers you could make to your customers that will save them money. If they have bought from you through your website, could you email them a unique code that will give them a personal discount off their next order? What about a free extended warranty or insurance? For inspiration, check out what other organizations in your industry are offering their customers and then explore what you could do that would be even better.

2 Run a testimonial-gathering exercise

Contact past and present customers and offer them the chance to win a prize for completing the phrase 'I love dealing with [your company] because . . .'. There could be different categories, for example the most original testimonial, the wittiest, the most appealing and so on. Award prizes for each category and publish a selection of the testimonials on your website. This activity will also make a good press release.

3 Put mirrors in front of your telephone staff

Invest in free-standing mirrors, but not with a magnifying lens, and position them so that your customer support staff can see their own reflections when they are talking to customers on the telephone. This will encourage them to smile, which will make them sound friendlier on the phone. There are also several other benefits of smiling – see Sunday's chapter to remind yourself of what they are.

4 Put on an event

Invite your customers to an event, such as a treasure hunt on a Sunday afternoon. This could be on foot or it could take the form of a car rally in which clues have to be solved. Tell them that they are welcome to bring along family and friends, and that there will be prizes for the winners. This type of event has a wide appeal, is relatively inexpensive to run and provides an opportunity to build good relationships with your customers in a relaxed atmosphere.

5 Give your customers an unexpected gift

This is one of the key routes to achieving customer excellence and need not be a costly option – see the example of the stationery supplier in Wednesday's chapter. The gift could accompany their next purchase or be sent to them as a thank you for referring a new customer to you.

6 Send birthday cards to your customers

Many organizations send out Christmas cards to their customers but very few send out birthday cards. These are unexpected and far more personal, and they demonstrate that you care. Recipients will be pleasantly surprised and feel that yours is a genuinely caring, 'thoughtful' organization. The cost is minimal, but the value is huge.

7 Conduct a customer satisfaction survey

It is essential that you are in touch with your customers' views about your organization and that you willingly and positively respond to any complaints or suggestions that they make. Also, people like to be asked for their opinions – it makes them feel valued and keeps you uppermost in their minds. See Tuesday's chapter for ideas on what to include in a survey. There are online survey tools that you could utilize to conduct a survey by email.

8 Spring clean your business

Step into your customer's shoes and 'visit' your business, as if for the first time. Does it feel bright, warm and inviting? Does it feel like an organization you would enjoy doing business with? If not, why not? Experiment with making small changes – moving furniture around, updating displays or including an 'offer of the week' on your website. What would appeal to your customers and how can you supply it?

9 Go public with your customer care standards

People buy people first and if you are able to build a reputation as a customer-friendly organization, then customers will stay loyal to you. Monday's chapter focused on creating customer care standards while Saturday's chapter presented the idea of creating and rolling out a branded customer service programme. Going public on these initiatives will enhance your reputation significantly. Think of John Lewis's slogan, 'Never knowingly undersold', or Marks & Spencer's policy for exchanging unwanted goods.

10 Give awards to your outstanding staff

Recognize those members of your staff who, on their own initiative, 'go the extra mile' for customers. Some organizations nominate an employee of the month. Others give personal awards such as a dinner for two at a local, good-quality restaurant or a gift voucher that would be really appreciated by that particular individual. Whatever you choose to do, publicize it through your internal communications channels, e.g. your newsletter or intranet. Ideally, also include testimonials from customers relevant to the award winners.

Answers

Sunday: 1c; 2b; 3d; 4a; 5b.
Monday: 1c; 2b; 3d; 4b; 5b;
6a; 7d; 8b; 9a; 10c.
Tuesday: 1c; 2d; 3a; 4b; 5c;
6d; 7a; 8b; 9b; 10d.
Wednesday: 1d; 2b; 3a; 4c;
5b; 6d; 7a; 8b; 9c; 10d.

Thursday: 1b; 2d; 3c; 4a; 5d;
6a; 7b; 8c; 9a; 10d.
Friday: 1b; 2a; 3d; 4c; 5a; 6b;
7d; 8a; 9c; 10b.
Saturday: 1b; 2c; 3a; 4d; 5a;
6b; 7d; 8a; 9c; 10b.

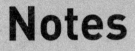

Notes

LEARN IN A WEEK,
WHAT THE EXPERTS
LEARN IN A LIFETIME

For information about other titles
in the series, please visit
www.inaweek.co.uk